Apostolic Letters of Faith, Hope, and Love

 Galatians, 1 Peter, and 1 John

BRUCE M. METZGER

Cascade Books

A division of *Wipf & Stock Publishers*

199 West 8th Avenue, Suite 3 • Eugene OR 97401

APOSTOLIC LETTERS OF FAITH, HOPE, AND LOVE
Galatians, 1 Peter, and 1 John

ISBN 10: 1-59752-501-4
ISBN 13: 978-1-59752-501-5

Cataloging-in-publication data

Metzger, Bruce Manning.
Apostolic letters of faith, hope, and love : Galatians, 1 Peter, and 1 John / Bruce M. Metzger.

xiv + 96 p.; 20.3 cm.

Eugene, Ore.: Cascade Books, 2006

ISBN 10: 1-59752-501-4   (alk. paper)
ISBN 13: 978-1-59752-501-5

1. Bible. N.T. Epistles—Criticism, interpretation, etc. 2. Bible. N.T. Galatians. 3. Bible. N.T. 1 Peter. 4. Bible. N.T. 1 John. I. Title.

BS2636 M47 2006

Apostolic Letters of
Faith, Hope, and Love

Contents

Abbreviations

GTS	Gettysburg Theological Studies
HTR	*Harvard Theological Review*
IBC	Interpretation: A Bible Commentary for Teaching and Preaching
ICC	International Critical Commentary
ISBE	*International Standard Bible Encyclopedia.* 5 vols. Edited by James Orr. Grand Rapids: Eerdmans, 1939
IVPNTCS	IVP New Testament Commentary Series
j.	Jerusalem Talmud (Yerushalmi)
JBL	*Journal of Biblical Literature*
JEA	*Journal of Egyptian Archaeology*
JR	*Journal of Religion*
JSNT	*Journal for the Study of the New Testament*
JSNTSup	Journal for the Study of the New Testament Supplement Series
KJV	King James Version
LCL	Loeb Classical Library
LEC	Library of Early Christianity
MNTC	Moffatt New Testament Commentary
NICNT	New International Commentary on the New Testament
NIGTC	New International Greek Testament Commentary
NovT	*Novum Testamentum*
NovTSup	Novum Testamentum Supplements
NRSV	New Revised Standard Version
NTC	New Testament in Context
NTR	New Testament Readings
NTS	*New Testament Studies*
NTT	New Testament Theology
PSQ	*Political Science Quarterly*
RSR	*Religious Studies Review*
RSV	Revised Standard Version
SacPag	Sacra Pagina
SBLDS	Society of Biblical Literature Dissertation Series
SBLRBS	Society of Biblical Literature Resources for Biblical Studies

SBLSBS	Society of Biblical Literature Sources for Biblical Studies
SJT	*Scottish Journal of Theology*
SNTSMS	Society for New Testament Studies Monograph Series
t.	Tosefta
WBC	Word Biblical Commentary
WTJ	*Westminster Theological Journal*
WUNT	Wissenschaftliche Untersuchungen zum Neuen Testament
ZAW	*Zeitschrift für die alttestamentliche Wissenschaft*
ZNW	*Zeitschrift für die neutesstamentliche Wissenschaft und die Kunde der älteren Kirche*

Preface

"FAITH, HOPE, and love . . . and the greatest of these is love." So wrote the apostle Paul to the church at Corinth (1 Cor 13:13). What Paul and two other apostolic writers had to say about these three central elements of the Christian religion still has relevance and meaning for believers today.

The following pages set forth the teaching from three of the twenty-one letters contained in the New Testament: Galatians, 1 Peter, and 1 John. Each letter presents characteristic emphases of three prominent leaders in the early church: Paul, Peter, and John. Each letter arises out of quite different social and theological backgrounds, and each provides insight into the manner in which the special needs of the recipients of the letter were met. Key words and phrases from each letter are discussed within the context of the occasion that called forth the writing of the letter. At the same time the theological and devotional import of the writer's teaching is related to the Christian life, then and now. A concluding chapter weaves together theological and ethical themes common to the three principal strands of New Testament Christianity.

Faith puts us on the path;

hope keeps us walking;

and love is what the Christian life is all about.

Introduction

Letters and Epistles

A DISTINCTION IS often made between the terms "letter" and "epistle." Letters, as Adolf Deissmann (1866–1937) repeatedly emphasized, were generally private missives and dealt with circumstances of the passing moment.[1] Confidential and personal in nature, they were intended only for the person or persons to whom they are addressed. Epistles, however, were on a more sophisticated level of literary effort, and were written with the intention of being both public and more or less permanent. In brief, the letter is a slice of life, while the epistle is a product of literary art.

The examples in the New Testament combine features of both the letter and the epistle. The letters of Paul are all real letters, arising from real situations in his life or the lives of those to whom he writes. At the same time, they are quasi-official letters from an apostle rather than merely private letters, and their style is more formal than the ephemeral letters preserved among the Greek papyri.[2]

Some of the other letters in the New Testament are more akin to the form and style of a theological treatise (for example, 1 Peter and 1 John). Even these, however, were not originally directed to every congregation in the ancient Mediterranean, but were intended for particular—even if loosely defined—destinations, and were written in order to deal with urgent difficulties experienced by the recipients,

[1] Deissmann, *Light from the Ancient East*, 233–45.

[2] See, for example, Meecham, *Light from Ancient Letters*; and White, "Greek Letter Writing."

such as persecution, heresy, and religious or moral laxity. Thus the New Testament letters incorporate elements of the ongoing life of the congregations, such as liturgical materials, moral guidelines, and religious instruction applicable to many believers in addition to the immediate recipients.

Furthermore, it should be noted that the literary form of a letter/epistle combines the advantages of a conversation and a treatise. In such a format it is possible to communicate truth, not only abstractly, but in close relation to the personal circumstances of the readers.

Classification of New Testament Letters

Of the twenty-seven documents that comprise the New Testament, twenty-one are in the format of a letter. Of these, fourteen have been traditionally attributed to Paul, and the other seven to a variety of other authors. As regards the Pauline letters, the titles now given to them involve the names of the recipients (To the Romans, To the Galatians, To Philemon, etc.), whereas for the others, called the General or Catholic Letters, the titles identify the author (Letter of James, Letter of Jude, etc.). These titles, it goes without saying, were added by scribes and editors after the several letters had been collected into a corpus.

The Pauline letters are in two series: those addressed to churches are followed by those addressed to individual recipients. In both cases the sequence of the letters has very little practical utility; they are arranged roughly according to length, the longest (Romans) standing first and the shortest (Philemon) last. As it happens, in this order the nine letters to seven churches fall into one group, and the four letters to individuals fall into another group.

In almost all manuscripts of the complete Greek New Testament the General Letters follow Acts and precede the Pauline Letters, whereas in Latin manuscripts the Pauline

Letters often precede the General Letters. This latter sequence is generally followed in English Bibles.

The Form of Ancient Letters

The form of an ancient Greco-Roman letter was conspicuously different from the modern letter.[3] At its beginning one finds the sender's name, followed by that of the recipient, and a short salutation. The message in the body of the letter was often introduced by an appeal to the gods in terms of gratitude or thanksgiving or of a prayer for the welfare of the recipient. At the end of the letter came the conveyance of greetings.

The apostle Paul's letters, while they fall within the category of such Hellenistic letters, show some developments of the letter pattern based on the apostle's creativity. Identification of the writer (co-workers are sometimes named) and of the addressees is followed by expanded descriptions of both parties in terms of their standing in relation to God through Christ. Specifically, the stereotyped Hellenistic "Greetings!" (χαίρειν) is replaced by "Grace to you and peace from God our Father and the Lord Jesus Christ."

The conclusion of Paul's letter often contains personal news and a final greeting. This is never the ordinary Greek "Farewell" (ἔρρωσθε, as in Acts 15:29), but a characteristic blessing, "The grace of our Lord Jesus Christ be with you."

In one or another respect, the General Letters (but not 1 John) adopt several of Paul's innovations in letter writing. Most of them are addressed not to a single Christian community but generally to several or to all. They are less like personal letters than most of Paul's, and more like of-

---

[3]   See, for example, Doty, *Letters in Primitive Christianity*; Stowers, *Letter Writing in Greco-Roman Antiquity*; and White, "New Testament Epistolary Literature."

ficial letters or sermons from a bishop or elder to a group of churches.

Without deprecating the very great role the apostle Paul played as a leader and theologian, it must be said that the General Letters supply evidence for the development of a rich and broad leadership within the early Christian communities.

The Manner of Writing Letters

In antiquity, just as today, people sometimes wrote letters personally and sometimes they dictated to a secretary or amanuensis.[4] In the latter case, one might dictate slowly word by word, with the amanuensis writing each word verbatim. Or one might dictate more rapidly with the message being taken down stenographically. In this case the material would, of course, need to be transcribed again. Besides dictating word by word, there was also the practice of giving the amanuensis exact instructions about the content of the letter and leaving the choice of wording to the amanuensis.

In the case of his letter to the Romans, we know that Paul dictated it to a certain Tertius, who added his own greeting among those that Paul was sending (Rom 16:22). In three other letters the apostle mentions explicitly that he has written the final greeting with his own hand, presumably as a guarantee of genuineness (1 Cor 16:21; Col 4:18; and especially 2 Thess 3:17). Near the close of his Letter to the Galatians Paul adds an autographic postscript, "See with what large letters I am writing to you with my own hand" (Gal 6:11). Since the subject matter changes at this

---

[4]   Bahr, "Paul and Letter Writing in the First Century"; Longenecker, "Ancient Amanuenses and the Pauline Epistles"; Harry Y. Gamble, "Amanuensis"; see also Tait, "The Strategi and Royal Scribes"; and White, *Light from Ancient Letters,* 215–16.

point, it is probable that here he has taken the stylus from the amanuensis.

How far the New Testament contains letters for which a secretary had some responsibility for the language and style has been debated. It is possible that this is how we should understand the comment made near the close of 1 Peter: "By Silvanus, a faithful brother as I regard him, I have written briefly to you" (1 Pet 5:12).

The Dispatch and Delivery of Letters

In antiquity there was no organized postal service available for the general populace.[5] The system of letter carriers created by the emperor Augustus (the *cursus publicus*) was restricted to the dispatch of government communiqués from Rome to officials in the provinces. Private individuals, therefore, had to make their own arrangements for the carrying and delivery of letters.[6] Wealthy families would keep a certain number of slaves to serve as couriers. Families and friends living near one another would pool their couriers in order to increase the opportunities to get off or receive a letter. But there were never enough carriers to meet the needs, and delays were inevitable. The opposite side of the coin was the need to dash off some lines at breakneck speed in order to take advantage of an available courier.

The actual transmission of private letters was exposed to many uncertainties, delays, and, at times, almost insuperable difficulties. Travel whether by land or by sea could be hazardous.[7] In all the countries referred to in the New

[5] Westermann, "On Inland Transportation and Communication in Antiquity"; Zilliacus, *From Pillar to Post: The Troubled History of the Mail*; and White, *Light from Ancient Letters,* 214–15.

[6] McGuire, "Letters and Letter Carriers in Christian Antiquity"; and Mitchell, "New Testament Envoys."

[7] Casson, *Travel in the Ancient World.*

Testament (except Egypt) the terrain is mountainous. One could travel by land, of course, only by daylight. The rigors of winter prevented travel by sea as well as by land. There was also the ever-present possibility of being waylaid by bandits or by pirates. Then too, illness or accident might incapacitate the one who was carrying the letter. It is not surprising to find in antiquity occasional reference to letters written but never received. Others were lost for months, or even years, before finally being delivered. Through a series of mishaps, for example, a letter written by St. Augustine of Hippo in North Africa to St. Jerome in Bethlehem took nine years to be delivered!

Assessment

The letters in the New Testament deal with issues that belong to a particular period in the history of the church. At the same time, the treatment of the several problems that elicited a response on the part of Paul, Peter, John, and other leaders in the early church often involved exposition of fundamental teachings of the Christian faith. Thus it came about that these letters—having been recopied and circulated to other congregations, and finally collected together—eventually were incorporated among the primary documents of the Christian religion.[8]

Like the genre of gospels, the letters in the New Testament represent something new and original in the literature of their time. Sophisticated literary epistles, such as those of Cicero[9] or Seneca,[10] and the incidental papyrus let-

---

[8]   See Metzger, *The Canon of the New Testament.*

[9]   Cicero, *Letters to Quintus and Brutus; Letter Fragments; Letter to Octavian; Invectives; Handbook of Electioneering.*

[10]   Seneca, *Epistulae morales ad Lucilium.*

ters preserved in the dry climate of Egypt are well known.[11] But never before had the world ever seen anything quite like these rather lengthy letters/epistles, almost wholly concerned, not just with personal details, but with matters of Christian doctrine and conduct. Even the preliminary greeting and the concluding farewell are new and distinctively Christian formulas. If we ask what it was that provided the new dynamic behind the writing of these apostolic letters, the answer must certainly include reference to the several writers' loyal commitment to one whom they called "the Lord Jesus Christ."

[11] See, for example, Meecham, *Light from Ancient Letters*; and White, *Light from Ancient Letters,* 23–186.

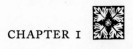

CHAPTER I

Paul's Epistle to the Galatians

Part Two: Into the Future

A Letter of Faith

GALATIA IS part of Asia Minor—what is now Turkey. The Galatian people were ethnically Gauls. That is to say, their ancestors had come from the region we know as France. The language that their ancestors had used—and perhaps they still made use of it—was the Gallic language, related to Irish and Welsh.

In the third and second centuries BC there were migrations of Gallic people from France, going eastward, crossing over into Asia, and settling in the central part of Asia Minor. They were ruled by native Gallic rulers. And then in 25 BC the last of their native rulers died, and the Roman government moved in and made Galatia a Roman province. It was no longer an independent kingdom; it became part and parcel of the approximately thirty Roman provinces.

This area was evangelized by Paul and Barnabas (AD 48–49), on the first missionary journey that the apostle Paul took (see Acts 13–14). He probably touched upon the southern part of the province of Galatia. Subsequently he made a second and a third missionary journey (see Acts 15:36—18:17; and 18:18—20:6). And it was also on one of those subsequent journeys that he had bad news as to the situation of the churches that he had founded previously in Galatia. He had heard the bad news that some Jewish Christian believers from Jerusalem had gone north and then west into Asia Minor and were beginning to unsettle the religious convictions of the Christians in Galatia by telling these people—most of whom were of Gentile background—that they were not really Christians unless they agreed to abide by the Old Testament precepts: to eat only kosher food, submit to the ritual act of circumcision, and observe the various feast days prescribed in the Old Testament. In short, these Jewish Christians from Jerusalem of the Pharisaic-type were telling these Gentiles in Galatia: *You cannot become a Christian unless you enter the church by way of the vestibule of the synagogue.*

Paul heard troubling rumors of how his converts were now wondering *Are we second-class Christians? Must we observe all the Old Testament precepts, not merely the Ten Commandments?*[1] We can understand that Paul was very seriously distressed at hearing this. He sets out at once to write a letter, since he could not retrace his steps at the moment, and to try to correct these aberrations of Christian teachings and the false doctrines that were being sown among congregations that he had helped to found on a previous visit. The occasion for the writing of this brief letter was Paul's concern that these Christians were slipping back again, and were becoming, not Christians who put their trust only in the Lord Jesus Christ, but who put their trust also in what they might do to earn their standing in addition to having faith in Christ.

In interpreting the Bible, we must naturally be careful to interpret everything that is said. But now and then—and I say this with caution—we can be alerted by what is not

---

[1] It is noteworthy that 613 commandments were identified by the school of Rabbi Akiba; later, in the Babylonian Talmud, Rabbi Simlai remarks: "613 commandments were revealed to Moses at Sinai, 365 being prohibitions equal in number to the solar days, and 248 being mandates corresponding in number to the limbs of the human body" (*b. Makkot* 23b). Jewish rabbinical scholars had enumerated 613 "commandments" in the Old Testament: 365 prohibitions (negative formulations) and 348 commands (positive formulations).

said. Of course, there is nothing in this letter about television and one cannot draw any kind of conclusion because Paul says nothing specifically about television. But we see that in every one of his other letters Paul begins by giving thanks (see Rom 1:8-17; 1 Cor 1:4-9; 2 Cor 1:3-7; Phil 1:3-11; Col 1:3-8; 1 Thess 1:2-10). He thanks even what God has done at Corinth, in spite of all the troubles that were being fomented in that city. When we see that only in this letter does he plunge right into an attempt to set his readers straight without his usual initial paragraph of thanksgiving, I think it is legitimate to draw a conclusion from what is not said. In this case, Paul is so much exercised that his beloved converts are slipping away that he cannot even think of one thing for which to give thanks to God.

It is very easy to outline this letter of six chapters because it falls neatly into three different sections. In chapters 1 and 2, Paul speaks about historical background. Chapters 3 and 4 are devoted primarily to theology. Chapters 5 and 6 deal chiefly with ethics.

The writer begins with the salutation similar to his salutation in other letters. But following the salutation is no paragraph of thanksgiving. The next words are a parenthesis. Some English versions use parentheses. The NRSV uses dashes: "Paul an apostle—sent neither by human commission nor from human authorities, but through Jesus Christ and God the Father, who raised him from the dead—" (Gal 1:1). That is the close of the parenthesis. So the salutation itself would be, "Paul an apostle," and we skim through the parenthetical words, "Paul an apostle . . . and all the members of God's family who are with me, To the churches of Galatia." This is the normal way that hundreds of other ancient letters begin. The name of the author (the writer) and the name of the recipient. There is no street address, not even a city, because the person carrying the letter would have received information that would enable him or her to go to that particular place and to give the letter to the designated recipient(s).

Paul then proceeds to the greeting: "Grace to you and peace from God our Father and the Lord Jesus Christ, who gave himself for our sins to set us free from the present evil age, according to the will of our God and Father; to whom be the glory, for ever and ever. Amen" (Gal 1:3-5).

One way to read a letter is to try to analyze from what is said what is being answered. If you hear somebody on the telephone, you catch, of course, only what that individual is saying. You must piece together from the tenor of what has been said what the person on the other end of the line is saying, or complaining about, or questioning. In the letters of the New Testament, if a writer denies something—makes a negative statement—it is possible, in fact it may be probable, that such a denial is directed against some statement that has been made that requires some kind of correction. Paul an apostle—sent neither by human commission nor from human authorities . . . ." His detractors were probably saying that Paul is a second-rate apostle, because he is not among the Twelve whom Jesus selected in the days of his flesh. Paul's detractors were probably saying that his authority is not on the same level with the authority of the Twelve. And so these Pharisaically-minded people from Jerusalem, these Jewish Christians, were sowing seeds of dissension, saying to the Galatians: *The preacher you have heard is a second-rate apostle. He was not chosen by Jesus Christ in the days of his flesh.* However that might be, the main point here is that Paul is affirming that his apostleship is not of human origin but was a divine commission. He was not made an apostle by a group of people, not "by human commission"—not from synod, or presbytery, or conference. Nor was his commission given to him by a bishop, by a supervisor, by a plurality of people, or by a single individual human being. He is an apostle "neither by human commission nor from human authorities"; but he is an apostle "through Jesus Christ." And he will later (in chapters 1 and 2) emphasize that they can rely on him as being on a par with these pillars of the church in Jerusalem because he, like them, was also called by Jesus Christ.

The salutation, "Grace to you and peace" (1:3) is similar to the salutation in every other New Testament letter. What a magnificent way to begin a letter. None of the ancient pagan letters has anything like the magnificence of "Grace to you, and peace." Peter uses the same phrase, adding "mercy." This is the way the Christians learned to write their letters. Notice that Paul never says, "Peace be to you, and grace." He always put grace first: "Grace to you and peace." He did not sit down and figure this out mentally—it just came to him as the most appropriate thing in the world. Our standing rests only on the goodness, the love, the compassion, the grace of God. That is primary. And after that we have peace. "Grace to you and peace."

The New Testament speaks about having peace with God and enjoying the peace of God. These are the two sides: the objective and the subjective aspects of peace. Peace with God: hostility that existed because of our sin has been taken away. We have peace with God, objectively are at peace through Christ. Then we subjectively enjoy the peace of God. That tranquility, that calmness, that degree of downright satisfaction knowing that God is our heavenly Father. Peace with God—on this we can base the peace that we have of God. This is peace through "Jesus Christ, who gave himself for our sins to set us free," to rescue us, "from the present evil age"; and all of that is traced back to the sovereign "will of our God and Father, to whom be the glory for ever and ever" (1:4-5).

In the RSV and NRSV you will find a white line following v. 5 and before the opening of v. 6. That blank space is not an imperfection accidentally left by the printer because he failed to press the lines together. The blank space was deliberately left there. The RSV and NRSV translators thought not only that they would help the reader by paragraphing, but also here and there left a blank space (a white line) to indicate that a totally different subject matter followed.

So now with the preliminaries completed, Paul plunges right into the subject matter of his letter. And he does so without pausing to give thanks for anything. He begins by declaring, "I am astonished." This might be positive or it might be negative. What follows makes it abundantly clear that it is negative. "I am astonished that you are so quickly deserting him who called you in the grace of Christ" (1:6). That is a way of expressing dissatisfaction. *I am astonished that you are so quickly turning tail and becoming traitors to— that you are deserting—the one who called you.*

Who is it that calls us? Luther thought that the "him" in "deserting him who called you" means they were deserting Paul, going after other leaders. But Paul never anywhere indicates, in other parts of the letter, that he is the one who issued the call; it is the Deity. Does this mean then that "you are deserting Christ who called you"? No, it can hardly mean that, because of what follows, *deserting Christ who called you in the grace of Christ.* This is repetitious and must mean—for it is totally in harmony with Paul's way of thinking elsewhere—"deserting God." *God called you in the grace of Christ.*

Paul proceeds quickly, in the rest of chapter 1, to indicate that they are setting up a false gospel—which is not another one (1:6-7). And this gospel that he preaches, he says in v. 12, he did not receive "from a human source," but it came to him through a revelation of Jesus Christ.

He now enumerates, in the rest of chapter 1, the various times he was at Jerusalem, and therefore able to be in contact with the twelve apostles, or at least as many of them as remained there. He was there, he said, very briefly after his conversion on the Damascus Road; he then went away into Arabia (v. 17). We are not told by Paul what he did there, but he probably meditated. He probably thought through the implications that God had called him on the Damascus Road, not because of good works that Paul had done—in fact, he was persecuting the church of Jesus Christ. He called him only because God's will and purpose wanted to make of Paul a chosen vessel to bring the Gospel to the Gentiles. Then, after three years, he did visit Cephas (or Peter), but only for two weeks (v. 18). They talked together about various things, but not a long enough time for Peter to give Paul a thorough rundown of all of Christian theology. No, Paul had received this, he says, from Jesus Christ.

In chapter 2 he says that fourteen years later he again went to Jerusalem. He is attempting to show, on the basis of his earlier history, how infrequently he had been with the twelve apostles, and had, therefore, no chance to become their understudy, to be subordinate to them. When he had a conference with them, they acknowledged that he was on a par with them. He says that after he had told them the content of his theological presentation, they—that is, Peter and James and John—"recognized the grace that had been given to me" (v. 9a). Then those three leaders "gave to Barnabas and me the right hand of fellowship" (v. 9b). No longer was Paul afraid of being given "the left foot of fellowship." No, he is welcomed; he is given "the right hand of fellowship." And they say, *What you are preaching is totally in harmony with what we have been preaching. You go forward, now, and carry this message to the Gentiles; we will carry it to the Jewish people.* Only, they said, be sure to "remember the poor" (v. 10).

The church at Jerusalem was in a poverty-stricken condition. The earliest stage in the church, according to the book of Acts (see especially Acts 2 and 4), was an experiment in Christian communism, when people had everything in common, and real estate was sold, and the money used to support the poor.[2] During the subsequent famine in the 40s, and again later throughout the Roman Empire, there was a very severe economic depression. Paul raised a collection from Gentile Christian believers to give back to the "mother church" at Jerusalem. We read in the epistles to the Corinthians how he, along with others, carried this money (1 Cor 16:1-4; 2 Cor 8:1—9:15). He did not go by himself; he got two other people, among those who had contributed liberally, to go with him, to make sure the total amount was given over to the people in Jerusalem. He said he was eager to do that very thing.

Paul had psychology as well as Christian charity behind him. He knew that if you raise a generous collection of money from Gentile Christian believers, it might somehow indirectly stop the mouths of Jewish Christian believers, who were all the time harping that the Gentile Christian believers were second-rate. I think you can understand what the psychology would be: if they've received a lot of money from Gentile Christian believers, it would behoove other believers not to complain too severely about their theology.

Finally, chapter 2 concludes by saying "But when Cephas," that is Peter, "came to Antioch" (2:11). One has to switch gears geographically. Up to this point, Paul has been saying how infrequently he went to Jerusalem, "the mother church." Consider Antioch—north of Palestine, in Syria, a Gentile and Jewish center, a crossroads, a "mixing-pot."[3] He is talking now about Peter, who had gone north; Paul had returned to Antioch, the first missionary-sending church. And the two of them have a conference at Antioch. While

---

[2] Bartchy, "Community of Goods in Acts."

[3] Norris, "Antioch of Syria"; and Sandwell and Huskinson, editors, *Culture and Society in Later Roman Antioch*.

Peter had been living there at Antioch, he would have table-fellowship with Gentile Christian believers.[4] He ate meals with them and participated in the Lord's Supper with them. Now when people from Jerusalem, Jewish Christian believers, go up to Antioch, Peter begins to think a little bit: *I will fall out with them if I continue this open fashion that I have of eating and fraternizing with Gentile Christian believers.* These were very strict, Pharisaically-minded, Jewish Christian believers that had come north from Jerusalem. So Paul notices that more and more Peter withdraws himself. And then there is an altercation between Paul and Peter. "But when I saw that they were not acting consistently with the truth of the gospel, I said to Cephas before them all, 'If you, though a Jew, live like a Gentile and not like a Jew, how can you compel the Gentiles to live like Jews?'" (2:14). That is, how can he require them to be obedient to the Old Testament precepts?

We here come to a watershed in the early Christian church. A watershed on the earth's surface is, you know, that place that is up in the mountains—it is a dividing line. Northern New York State is such a watershed. Some rain falling at this spot trickles into little rivulets that finally enter into the St. Lawrence River, emptying into the north Atlantic Ocean. Other raindrops, falling only a few feet south, fall on the other side of the watershed, and find their way into rivers, emptying into the Ohio River, and then the Mississippi River; and finally, those raindrops ultimately land in the Gulf of Mexico, hundreds and hundreds of miles distant! At first they were very close together. So doctrinally, in the early church, there seemed very little difference. But the Jewish Christian believers said, *In order to attain salvation, you must be obedient to the Old Testament commands:*

---

[4] Bartchy, "Table Fellowship."

the ritual act of circumcision, not eating pork chops, obeying all the rituals, and believe in Jesus Christ; then you'll be saved.

Paul, on the other hand, said, *You are saved by faith alone. You are saved by Jesus Christ, apart from trying to earn your redemption. Then you are obedient to God's will as expressed in the Old Testament. Morally, you must be in accordance with the Ten Commandments. Ceremonially, these have been blotted out.* A very little difference, but a difference of sequence. How different the church would be today if the point of view of these Pharisaically-minded Christian believers from Jerusalem had prevailed.

In that case, you and I would be part of an institution that is nationalistically bound to the Jewish race. You and I would not belong to an international Christian church. You and I could not celebrate the Lord's Supper by what we might call "open communion"—all those who believe in Christ—but only those who had submitted to the Jewish ritual of circumcision. This is a very important time in the early Christian community, and it is settled by Paul, under the guidance of the Spirit. He does this in the way in which—without relaxing the Old Testament—Jesus Christ is exalted.

The argument begins in chapter 3 on a personal level (3:1-5). He commences on the level of asking: *Well, consider your own experience, you Gentile Galatian converts. Did you receive the gift of the Holy Spirit because you had observed the Old Testament commands, or through faith in Jesus Christ?* Now that is a kind of a rhetorical question. He knows what their answer must be. Namely, it was through responding in faith to the preaching of the gospel that they received the gift of the Spirit, that the Spirit had given them the powers of working miracles and wonders, and had begun their Christian faith. So he asks, secondly, "Having started with the Spirit, are you now ending with the flesh?" (3:3).

After this brief introduction on the basis of their asking themselves what their own experience had been, Paul turns for the rest of chapter 3 to a biblical argument. He begins by saying, *Consider the case of Abraham.* "Just as Abraham 'believed God, and it was reckoned to him as righteousness'" (3:6; see Gen 15:6; Rom 4:16). That is to say, Abraham became right in the sight of God not because he was circumcised. No, the law of Moses regarding circumcision came 430 years after Abraham. It was on the basis of his trust and commitment to God that God recognized Abraham as the father of the faithful.

So he then says, "For all who rely on works of the law are under a curse" (3:10). Here Paul goes to another part of the Pentateuch. Having begun in Genesis, he now turns to the book of Deuteronomy, where he reminds them of the statement that, "Cursed is everyone who does not observe and obey all the things written in the book of the law" (Deut 27:26). Now he says, *No one is ever able to keep all of them. So all alike fall under the reproach of having violated God's holy laws.* This goes far beyond the Ten Commandments—for the Jewish rabbis had counted 613 commandments in the Old Testament, all of which were to be obeyed.

The next stage of Paul's theological argument in Galatians 3 concerns tackling the very thorny question of what the Gentile is to do about the Old Testament. He has already quoted a passage concerning Abraham from Genesis. He has also quoted Deuteronomy 27:26. He has to make a case to show that the Old Testament still remains as a guide for the Christian Gentile believer. But at the same time, its ceremonial laws are set aside. How does he do this?

Paul asks the question, "Why then the law?" (3:19). That is, up to this point he is trying to show that it is not by observing the commands of the Old Testament law that a person becomes right in the sight of God. He answers his question, and he answers it in a very concise way: The law was added 430 years after Abraham had received the promise "that all the Gentiles shall be blessed in you" (3:8; Gen 12:3). Why did God add that law to his promise given to Abraham? Paul says it was added because of transgressions. Until the offspring should come to whom the promise had been made. Namely, in you and in your seed, your offspring, shall all of the nations be blessed. It was ordained by angels through an intermediary (3:19).

This is an aspect of Jewish theology not mentioned in the Old Testament. Namely, Jewish people by this time considered that God gave the Old Testament law to angels, and they in turn delivered it to Moses on Mt. Sinai.[5] Not only Paul mentions this, but Stephen mentions it in Acts (7:38, 53), and the unknown author of the Epistle to the Hebrews mentions as well that the holy and ineffable supreme God was so far removed that he did not come into personal contact with Moses in delivering the law, but delivered the law through an intermediary (Heb 2:2). Our author here uses this argument to denigrate the station of the law. It was even below the dignity of God to give it personally to Moses.

> Is the law then opposed to the promises of God? Certainly not! For if a law had been given that could make alive, then righteousness would indeed come through the law. But the scripture has imprisoned all things under the power of sin that what was promised through faith in Jesus Christ might be given to those who believe." (3:21-22)

Not to those who vainly try to keep the precepts of the law.

Now the author uses an illustration. He has quoted several times from the Old Testament. Now he uses what

---

[5] See, for example, *Jubilees* 1:27-29; 2:1; *Testament of Dan* 6:2; Philo, *On Dreams* 1.141; and Josephus, *Antiquities* 15.5.3.

might be called an example: "Now before faith came, we were imprisoned and guarded under the law until faith would be revealed. Therefore the law was our disciplinarian [*paidagōgos*] until Christ came, so that we might be justified by faith" (3:23-24). The Greek word here, *paidagōgos*, is very difficult to render into English because we do no have the function of a *paidagōgos* any longer in our culture.[6] The King James translators translated *paidagōgos* as our "schoolmaster," who brings us to Christ. Perhaps "custodian" or even "truant officer" would be a little more accurate. A *paidagōgos* was a slave who had charge of a child, taking the child daily from the home to the school where the tutor taught the child. The *paidagōgos* was not an instructor in the official sense of schoolmaster; there the King James translators were not quite accurate. He was a kind of guide or crossing guard at the place where the traffic was heavy, and the crossing guard at school time has to hold up a sign saying traffic must stop. In other words, he looked after the welfare of the child on the way to the schoolhouse.

Among the people of antiquity, *paidagōgos* got very bad press. There are some plays that say in a humorous sort of way, *You have such a sour face. You look just like a paidagōgos.* That is to say, the *paidagōgos* was always saying to the child, *Now, don't tarry. Don't get in the mud puddle there. Come on. Watch yourself. Hurry up, we'll be late.* The *paidagōgos* was always reproaching, was saying, *Don't do this; don't do that.* And so in a sense this was a very appropriate kind of illustration for Paul to use here when he says: Now the law was our *paidagōgos.* And we were kept under restraint while we were yet minors, children. "But," he says in v. 27, "now that faith has come, we are no longer under a disciplinarian, for in Christ Jesus you are all children of God though faith." In

[6] Young, "*Paidagogos*: The Social Setting of a Pauline Metaphor"; and Hanson, "The Origin of Paul's Use of *Paidagogos*."

other words, here his argument is that the law is temporary. And now that the Galatians have had faith in Christ, they are no longer under the tutelage and supervision of this custodian, the *paidagōgos*.

Let me try to summarize this part of Paul's argument by using the three words that Martin Luther used in condensing the theological argument of this point in Galatians. He used in German three words that have a certain rhythm or jingle. The law, he said, of the Old Testament, is a *Regel*, a *Riegel*, and a *Spiegel*.[7] In German, *Regel* means a rule. Paul's argument here is that the Old Testament law is a kind of rule that even the Gentiles may follow and not be led astray. It is not a rule to guarantee that they will have redemption, but a rule for when you are in such a situation that you know what ought to be done. And if you do not have time carefully, methodically to look at the whole thing, a quick rule of thumb that will never lead you astray as to what is right ethically is to go to the law.

The law is not only a *Regel*, but also a *Riegel*. In German, *Riegel* means a curb—a kind of restraint for a horse that guides the horse and curbs it from jumping over the traces. Luther applied this to the nations. The Mosaic law says, "You shall not kill" (Exod 20:13). "You shall not commit adultery" (Exod 20:14). You shall not bear false witness" (Exod 20:16). These still remain, for Jew and Gentile alike, as a *Riegel*—as a curb against social anarchy.

Third—and here Martin Luther probes the particular argument that Paul uses and highlights here—the law of the Old Testament acts as a *Spiegel*, a mirror. He says, we look into the Old Testament law with its commands to see how far short you and I have fallen from being what God wants us to be. And being in that place of despondency, the law drives us to Christ, where alone we can find mercy.

[7] See also John Calvin, *Institutes of the Christian Religion*, II.7.6–17.

Now at the conclusion of chapter 3, with his argument to try to show that the Old Testament law still has some function, although in the ceremonial way no longer the requirement of circumcision—that has been replaced by baptism; no longer the celebration of Passover—Christ is our Passover; no longer the observance of the seventh day of the week—replaced now by the first day of the week, and so forth. But the moral law still remains as a *Regel*, a *Riegel*, and a *Spiegel*, having their function generally in society as a restraint and personally to show how much we need the forgiveness of God offered through Christ.

Now the apostle puts a knot in his argument here. He wraps it up in 3:28, saying, "There is no longer Jew or Greek, there is no longer slave nor free, there is no longer male and female; for all of you are one in Christ Jesus." *All of you Gentile believers in Galatia and we who were brought up in the synagogue and were Jews and now are Jewish Christians, you and we alike are one in Christ Jesus.*

In the Orthodox Jewish synagogue all faithful Jewish men pray three times daily. These are three prayers and benedictions out of a long series—it takes fifteen or eighteen minutes to go through the entire text even rapidly. "Blessed be He [God] that He did not make me a Gentile; blessed be He that He did not make me a boor [i.e., an ignorant peasant or a slave]; blessed be He that He did not make me a woman."[8] And in smaller type, if there are women in the Orthodox Jewish synagogue, they would be segregated; they would have to sit in the balcony. Then they are to say, "Blessed be He who has made me according to His will."

---

[8] See, for example, *Authorized Daily Prayer Book of the United Hebrew Congregations of the British Commonwealth of Nations,* 6–7. In *t. Berakot* 7.18 and *j. Berakoth* 13b, these benedictions are attributed to Rabbi Judah ben Elai (mid-second century AD); in *b. Menaḥoth* 43b, they are attributed to Rabbi Meier (also mid-second century AD).

How did this threefold benediction get into the Orthodox Jewish prayerbook? The same three items are mentioned in Galatians 3:28: "no longer Jew or Greek . . . no longer slave nor free . . . no longer male and female." Not only are these the same three, but the same three in the same sequence. You cannot believe that the maker of the Orthodox Jewish liturgy went to Paul's letter to the Galatians to get this. It could be a happenstance, but I don't think so. I think that the conservatism in the liturgy suggests that these prayers, at least that part of the daily prayers for all male Jews, goes back to a pre-Christian date. And that Rabbi Saul, before he became Paul the apostle, had been accustomed to pray in the synagogue those three prayers. And now, as a Christian believer, his mind and devotion runs through the same channels but with a different orientation. Now it is negated. In Christ "there is no longer Jew or Greek, there is no longer slave nor free, there is no longer male and female." Now with regard to race ("Jew and Greek"), with regard to society ("free and slave"), with regard to gender ("male and female")—in Christ Jesus they are all on a par. They are one in the sight of God, without differentiation. So he concludes this chapter: "If you belong to Christ, then you are Abraham's offspring, heirs according to the promise" (3:29).[9]

This leads Paul into chapter 4, where he develops a thought that I think would make a very good text for a Christmas sermon. Of course, one will want to use Matthew 2 and Luke 2 at Christmas. But what about now and then also preaching on Galatians 4:4-5? "But when the fullness of time had come, God sent his Son, born of a woman, born under the law, in order to redeem those who were under the law, so that we might receive the adoption as children."

[9] See Wiley, *Paul and the Gentile Women*.

"The fullness of time." They did not have watches or clocks. They had a *klepsydra*, a water clock. A *klepsydra* is a large vessel, made either of ceramic or metal, into which a trickle of water flows. And on the inner side of the vessel at various levels there are marks indicating, with the passage of time and the level of the water slowly rising, what this or that level might mean. For example, if court is to be convened at a particular hour, it would convene "in the fullness of time," when the level had reached that particular mark. Paul here is saying that God has a plan. And according to that plan, at the appropriate moment, in the great cosmic clock or *klepsydra,* then God sent forth his son into the world. In the fullness of time—he did not come just accidentally. He came totally in accord with God's plan. And when he came, he did not come to an outpost of the world's civilization. He came to the hub of three continents—Asia, Africa, and Europe—the little country of Palestine, the hub, from which there radiated highways to all parts of the then-civilized world. He came at the fullness of time, when the Roman people had brought about a period of peace—in Latin, the *Pax Romana*, the Roman peace: the two hundred years from 19 BC to AD 181, exactly two centuries, the longest period of general peace that the world had known or has known since. The Romans had unified the then-civilized world. Missionaries could go without let or hindrance over the highways, those good Roman roads, not hindered by warfare. The Greeks had been brought to the fullness of their time, and one language united all of the then-civilized world: the Greek language. The Jewish people, as well as the Romans and the Greeks, had been brought under the tutelage of God to their pinnacle through ethical monotheistic teaching—a prophet and lawgiver. And now through many synagogues, even Gentiles were beginning to imbibe something of the ethical monotheism taught by Israel. There was a fullness of time, an appropriate moment, and then, not accidentally, but according to God's plan, he sent his son.

His son was a gift, a present. God did not need to send him. God sent him "born of a woman, born under the law, in order to redeem those under the law, so that we might receive adoption." God had a plan. He gave a present. And this was for his people. There you have three points: Plan, Present, People. To redeem those that were under the law, that we might receive the adoption. Jews were under the law. Gentiles would be adopted into the family of God so that eventually there would be one people of God.

Later in chapter 4, Paul indicates in terms of reproof concerning the immaturity, spiritually speaking, of the Galatians. He says, They still want vainly to observe all kinds of Jewish fast days and new moons and seasons. "I am afraid," he says in 4:10 and 11, "that my work for you may have been wasted."

But now Paul beseeches them. He comes down, you might say, from his level of saying, *I am an Apostle; I have an authority, which was acknowledged by the leaders of the Jerusalem church: Peter, James and John. They gave me the right hand of fellowship. They did not create me an apostle. But they acknowledged that my apostleship was on their level.* Now he comes down and says, "I beg you, become as I am, for I also have become as you are" (4:12). Here he goes on to indicate, on the basis of friendship that they had had earlier with him, that they ought not to stand against him and his teachings.

The author then turns to an allegory of the Old Testament story of Sarah and Hagar. Sarah was the free-born wife of Abraham, and Hagar was his slave concubine. Teachers of the Bible generally warn students against allegorizing the scripture. Paul writes, "Now this is an allegory: these women are two covenants" (4:24). Martin Luther was right when he says that Paul, here, paints the house that he has already built.[10] Paul's argument is already firm, up to this point. Paul uses this illustration in order to decorate—in order to make more plain—the basic structure of the argument that has taken them thus far. Paul does not begin with allegory. He simply uses it now as an illustrative account at the end, when he says, "You who want to be under the law, to receive circumcision, to observe the Old Testament, kosher laws of diet, and so on, you are once again seeking to range yourselves with the children of Hagar, the slave woman." On the other hand, "Those who are believing in Christ, they are children of Sarah, who received the child of promise." He says, "But the Jerusalem above is free, and she is our mother" (4:26).

When you are seeking for a sermon appropriate for Mother's Day, the following could serve as a text for a Mother's Day sermon: "The Jerusalem above is free, and she is our mother." Of course, you need to say, in the context that Paul here is speaking about two ways of attaining redemption. Those who are the children, the offspring, so to speak, of Hagar, the slave woman, and those who are the offspring, spiritually speaking, of Sarah, the free woman. And he says here that the Jerusalem that is above—that is, the church—is free. The synagogue is enslaved to the Old Testament's ceremonial law. This Jerusalem above—the church—she is our mother.

The Roman Catholic Church, of course, has made much of this verse. It makes much of what Saint Cyprian, the church father in North Africa (martyred in AD 258 for his faith), said in one his letters: "Before we can have God as our Father, we must have the church as our mother."[11] At

---

[10] Martin Luther, *Lectures on Galatians 1535,* 433.

[11] *Habere non potest Deum patrem qui ecclesiam non habet matrem*; Cyprian, *The Unity of the Catholic Church,* chap. 6, Patrologia latina 4, 502.

first that may seem to put on its head everything that Paul has been saying in this chapter. And yet, I call it to your attention that John Calvin, in his *Institutes of the Christian Religion*, discusses Galatians 4:26. And, in brief, Calvin agrees with the general teaching, but not, irrevocably, its application: namely, that before we can have God as our Father, we must have the church as our mother.[12] It is only through the church that you and I learn about God and the gift of his beloved son, born at the fullness of time. We learn from our parents, who are in the church. We learn it from our pastor, who is in the church. We learn it, perhaps, reading the Bible, that has been transmitted through the church, and translated by Christian believers, and distributed by Bible societies. Even Robinson Crusoe on a desert island was not totally separated from the church, when, one day, he found washed up on the shore a sea-chest, and opening it, he discovered inside a copy of the Bible. That printed book put him in touch with the church and its message: "For God so loved the world that he gave his only Son, so that everyone who believes in him may not perish but may have eternal life" (John 3:16).

Yes, you and I know about Jesus Christ and God as our Father because of what we have learned through the instrumentality of believing people in the church, who came before us. So John Calvin says in his comment on this verse: "That unless we are obedient to the earthly church, and nourished by and through her, and reproved and chastened by her when we go wrong, we can never expect to be as the angels in heaven."[13]

The church is not only the mother of individuals, telling them this message of the gospel, and that God is waiting to be revealed as their Father, through Christ; but second, the

---

[12] Calvin, *Institutes of the Christian Religion*, 4.1.1.

[13] Calvin, *Galatians and Ephesians*.

church is the mother of very many charitable organizations that would not exist were it not for the church. Orphanages, hospitals, clinics, all kinds of social structures are in existence because they were born through those, as members of the church, who wanted to look after their fellow human beings. The church is our mother, and we as Protestants have a right, I think—as well as Roman Catholics, as well as the followers of Mary Baker Patterson Glover Eddy, and the Mother Church in Boston of Christian Science—we have a right, too, to look at this verse and to claim what is involved in it.

Chapters 5 and 6 of Galatians have to do with the application of this theology to everyday life. And very briefly, I concentrate now on 5:6: "For in Christ Jesus neither circumcision nor uncircumcision counts for anything; the only thing that counts is faith working through love." That is the only thing that is of avail in the sight of God. This repeats what he has been saying all over again: "We are justified by faith, not by works of the law." Of course, many people reading this are puzzled to read in the the letter of James, "faith without works is also dead" (James 2:26).

Those two verses are reconciled, and Paul and James are seen to be saying essentially the same thing, when we recognize that they are speaking about faith under different rubrics.[14] James talks about an intellectualized faith, a belief in certain doctrine. James says, "You believe that God is one . . . . Even the demons believe—and shudder" (James 2:19). That does not change them from their demonic status. They believe the fact that God exists, they have that kind of intellectualized faith. The kind of faith that Paul is talking about is not only intellectual but heart-commitment of one's life and soul to Jesus Christ as our savior. It is that kind of faith that is based on knowing who Christ is, but committing

[14] See, for example, Jeremias, "Paul and James."

oneself totally and entirely to him and to his saving power. It is that kind of faith working through love. Not a dead faith that stops with believing the creed, but a faith that involves a heart-commitment to Jesus Christ, that shows itself in daily living.

About the time of the Reformation, the following statement was coined, which I think shows the uniformity of the teaching of James and Paul: "We are saved by faith alone, but the faith that saves does not remain alone. It is followed by good works that testify to the reality of the faith." We are saved by faith alone, in Christ; but that kind of faith results—showing that it is a vital, living faith—in works of charity and good deeds, done now out of thankfulness for what God has given to you and me, not in order to earn our credit in the sight of God. We are saved by faith alone; but the faith that saves never remains alone.

What is the center of Pauline theology: the *centrum Paulinum*? If we had only the letter to the Galatians, and perhaps Romans, we might say that the central doctrine of Paul's thinking was justification by faith alone. But, of course, we have other works of his. And if we look throughout his correspondence, we will observe that in Galatians, and partly in Romans, Paul stresses the doctrine of justification by faith because, in those localities at that time, problems had emerged through Pharisaical Jewish Christian believers who were unsettling the faith of the Gentile Christian believers. And so, in that circumstance, Paul has to stress the relation of law and grace with regard to faith and works.

But if you look through all of these letters, I think you will agree with Adolf Deissmann, who pointed out that the phrase that occurs repeatedly in Paul's letters is the phrase "in Christ."[15] The Greek *en Christo* is a new kind of grammatical construction not used heretofore, the dative case of the name of a person, that you are "in" that person. Paul says again and again—in all of his letters, more than sixty times—"in Christ" or "in him." Nobody ever said, *I am in Plato*; nobody ever said, *I am in Moses*; it is impossible. But Jesus Christ as God's eternal son is divine, and so we and all believers can be "in him," who is God and man, who is human being and God. And so Paul invented a new Greek construction: the dative used in this unusual way that nobody else had thought of using, because, now for the first time, he has the possibility of speaking this way, since people now can be "in Christ." That is the *centrum Paulinum*, the center of Pauline theology. But so far as the Epistle to the Galatians is concerned, I think that we can say that in this letter, the central portion of Paul's teaching is faith.

> *Eternal God, who, in the fullness of time, sent forth thy Son, made of a woman, made under the law, that he might redeem those who are under the law, that we Gentiles might receive the adoption. Grant, we pray, that we may both study and know his holy word, that we may follow it day by day. We ask this in the name of Christ, who with thee and the Holy Spirit ever liveth, one God, world without end. Amen.*

[15] Deissmann, *Die neutestamentliche Formel "in Christo Jesus"*; idem, *St. Paul*, 135–57; see also Dunn, *The Theology of Paul the Apostle*, 390–412; and Schnelle, *Apostle Paul*, 290–92.

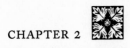

CHAPTER 2

The First Epistle of Peter

A Letter of Hope

THE FIRST epistle of Peter is shorter than Galatians: five chapters rather than six. It is a letter written in a totally different style, by a person whose background we are acquainted with because of the four gospels. It is attributed to this apostle, who had been chosen by Christ (*Come from the fishing boat, follow me*), by the one who later is regarded by the Roman Catholic Church, and to some extent, justifiably, as a prince of the apostles.

This letter of Peter, an apostle of Jesus Christ, begins in the same way as does the letter from Paul to the Galatians, with the author claiming to be an authoritative, divinely sent apostle. In 1:1 he addresses his letter, "To the exiles of the Dispersion," and then mentions five provinces: "in Pontus, Galatia, Cappadocia, Asia, and Bithynia." As you see, one of the provinces in Asia Minor was itself called "Asia." When one finds the word "Asia" in the New Testament (whether here, or in the book of Acts, or the book of Revelation), it never means the continent we know as Asia. Neither does it ever mean "Asia Minor." It always means the western tip of Asia Minor that comprised the province known as Asia, along with these four others, named Pontus, Galatia, Cappadocia, and Bithynia. Now that made up a motley crew of people that are being addressed by Peter; there were all kinds of native people: Asiatics, Greeks, Romans—slaves and free.

He is writing a general letter. That is the meaning of the "Catholic Epistles," those that are general, sent not to one locality alone—to Thessalonica, to Philippi, and so on. He is writing to the Christian exiles of the dispersion in these five different areas, and he says that these people—Christian believers from all kinds of ethnic backgrounds—are "chosen and destined." Now notice how he works in the Trinity: "destined by God the Father, and sanctified by the Spirit to be obedient to Jesus Christ, and to be sprinkled with his blood: May grace and peace be yours in abundance" (1:2). Again this stereotype plays that early Christians used, speaking about grace before our enjoyment of peace with God and the peace of God.

The author begins on this note and stresses throughout this letter the theme of hope. He speaks about hope in v. 3: "Blessed be the God and Father of our Lord Jesus Christ! By his great mercy he has given us a new birth into a living hope through the resurrection of Jesus Christ from the dead." He reiterates in 1:13: "set all your hope on the grace that Jesus Christ will bring you when he is revealed." And again in 1:21: "your faith and hope are set on God." Several other times in this letter he uses the noun "hope" and the verb "to hope." This letter, therefore, has deservedly been called "a letter of hope."

The epistle of Paul to the Galatians deals with a specific problem concerned with doctrine: whether Gentiles must become Jews before they can become Christians. The epistle that Peter writes to some of those same people in Galatia—as well as to Christians living in Pontus, Asia, Cappadoccia, Bithynia, and other areas in Asia Minor—was a different kind of problem. Their problem was not so much doctrine as a practical sort of problem. They were beginning to face the hot breath of the furnace of persecution. And Peter writes to them to encourage them how they may live consistent Christian lives in the face of a mounting wave of persecution not only from their neighbors but from their government as well. As we begin to look more particularly at 1 Peter, we see that the author is concerned to bring a note of hope to bear. They should not become despondent in the face of persecution. They should have hope and be encouraged that God, who has dealt with them generously in the past, will not forget them.

As was true in the case of Paul's letter to Galatia, this letter begins with the word "apostle." In Galatians, "Paul, an apostle of Jesus Christ"; here, "Peter, an apostle of Jesus Christ." A century ago, a philosopher and theologian in Denmark, Søren Kierkegaard, wrote a very interesting essay entitled "The Difference between an Apostle and a Genius." Now I don't know whether you would have thought of putting those two together and asking about the difference between them. This essay by Kierkegaard discusses the authority of an apostle. Why should people pay attention to what Paul says to the church of Galatia? We do not live there. Why should we pay attention to what Peter is saying to people who lived in Bithynia, in Pontus, and so on? What is the difference between an apostle and a genius? This essay, in case you are interested to read it in its entirety, is an appendix to Kierkegaard's book *The Present Age.*[1] The difference, he says, boils down to this: the genius belongs to this earthly domain, and the apostle gains his authority from the divine domain. The result of that difference is this: anyone who is judged to be a genius in one generation might well, five or six generations on, be eclipsed by someone greater. A genius is relative to the category of people among whom that person appears. A genius of a past generation, such as Michelangelo, in making a heavier-than-air "flying dove," as he called it, was surpassed in 1901 by Wilbur and Orville Wright, who made something still greater. But those who make the jumbo jets today are still higher up the ladder of being geniuses. Each one of these is surpassed; but an

---

[1]　Kierkegaard, *The Present Age.*

apostle is not surpassed. An apostle of Jesus Christ is not set aside by any future religious leader. And, therefore, even Einstein was bound to listen to what Paul, or Peter, or other apostles reported because they speak on behalf of God, and their authority remains through all the ages. They are never surpassed.

Paul might boast he has certain qualifications; but it is not because of those qualifications that you and I are to pay attention to him. Kierkegaard uses a rather humorous illustration. He said, let us suppose that Paul has a very great expertise in tentmaking or upholstery. Would we listen to him because he is a genius as an upholsterer? Of course not. And so, no matter what the expertise may be on the part of a human being here, that expertise is liable to be overtaken in another generation and that person set aside. But—and this is the main point I wish to make—an apostle of Jesus Christ is never set aside. And therefore the authority wielded by an apostle is not his own authority but speaks on behalf of the one who sent him. And, therefore, in these cases, we are to listen to Paul or to Peter because of whom they represent.

Now in the case of Peter, he did not have the kind of education that Paul had. Paul had been trained as a Jewish rabbi. Peter was a fisherman. He used a certain dialect when he spoke that made people recognize that: *Your speech betrays you. You're just a common working man, a fisherman; you have no education* (see Matt 26:73). And to the leaders in Jerusalem after Pentecost, Peter and John seemed to be ignorant and unlearned people (see Acts 4:13). The Greek of 1 Peter is some of the best Greek of all twenty-seven books in the New Testament, surpassed, I think, only by the epistle to the Hebrews with regard to elegance of Greek expression. This Greek is the result of the collaboration between Peter giving the authoritative teaching and his amanuensis (or scribe), Silvanus, who he says in 1 Peter 5:12, "Through Silvanus, whom I consider a faithful brother." And there

Peter discloses his secretary, the one who was taking down what Peter was telling him. And undoubtedly, Silvanus was giving to Peter's rough, untutored speech a more polished cast in syntax and vocabulary. Peter says, *I authorize this. And behind the words written now by Silvanus are the ideas that Jesus Christ gave to me. And you people in Pontus, Bithynia, Galatia, and so on, who receive this letter are to hear not the words of poor Peter, a bumbling fisherman. Not even the more polished expression of Silvanus, a faithful Christian brother as I regard him. But you are to hear the voice of Jesus Christ who speaks to you words of hope and comfort and encouragement. Therefore may grace and peace be multiplied to you.*

Now outlining this letter is somewhat more difficult than outlining the progression of Paul's letter to the Galatians. The latter was rather neat: the first two chapters, historical material; in the next two chapters, theological material; and the last two chapters, practical material. This letter of 1 Peter weaves together the doctrinal statements that are exhilarating to read along with practical application of the implications of Christian faith and life for everyday living in the home.

After saying we must rejoice in what God the Father of Jesus Christ has done, Peter first of all makes an appeal for Christian consistent living, an appeal for holiness in everyday living, starting with 1:13 and running to 2:10. He says, "set all your hope on the grace that Jesus Christ will bring you when he is revealed. Like obedient children, do not be conformed to the desire that you formerly had in ignorance. Instead, as he who called you is holy, be holy yourselves in all of your conduct" (1 Pet 1:13b-15).

Now the holiness he is speaking about here has to do not only with maintaining the right attitude in regard to consistent Christian living; but he speaks also of good works: "Conduct yourselves honorably among the Gentiles, so that, though they malign you as evildoers, they may see your honorable deeds and glorify God when he comes to judge" (2:12). These good works are not specially religious works of going to church and praying; that he has in mind as well. But the good works that he speaks about here are good works for the civic betterment of society, of looking with open eyes as to how you can help your neighbors—not necessarily only Christian neighbors, but how you can do good and treat well everyone alike. This is a very practical, a very down-to-earth kind of epistle.

This appeal to holiness of living comes to an end in that section that I just mentioned. Now he is speaking to this motley group of all kinds of ethnic tribes in that part of Asia Minor, and he tells them in 2:9, "You are a chosen race, a royal priesthood, a holy nation, God's own people." What a thrill many of these readers would have experienced. People who were outcasts, people who were slaves, people who did not amount to anything in the social pool—they never made a splash. These are people who felt despondent. This letter is to encourage them to have hope, to have confidence. Why? Because God has chosen them. "But you are a chosen race, a royal priesthood, a holy nation." So amid Jews and all types of Gentiles—whether members of this tribe or that tribe—those who are collected in the Christian church now form yet another group, and they are identified by Peter at this place as having been chosen by God.

What about these servants? These were men and women, slaves, meeting together before dawn to worship God, because in the daylight hours they would have to be about their masters' and mistresses' business. We learn about this situation in Bithynia, to which this letter goes. From a letter that comes to us early in the second century, written by the Roman governor of Bithynia, Pliny, who writes this letter in Latin to the emperor Trajan in Rome.[2] First Peter is a letter

---

[2] Stout, *Plinius, Epistulae*; and Sherwin-White, *The Letters of Pliny,*

that probably was written in the second half of the first century, and it would be the second generation of Christians in Bithynia with whom Pliny has to deal.

The problem was that the growth of the church in Bithynia in the early second century meant that fewer and fewer animals were being sold for sacrifice in the pagan temple. And this economic squeeze on the pagans who sold these animals meant that they were dead-set against the growth of the Christian church. It was taking business away from them. People did not buy as many animals for pagan sacrifice. So they went to Pliny the governor and said: *We must have a correction of this.* Pliny heard their pleas; and he called in Christians before his judgment seat. He also wrote to Trajan, the emperor, for further instruction. He wrote that he called before him various Christians, men and women. He tried to get them to confess what kind of crime they were perpetrating. He says in his letter to Trajan, *They don't seem to be doing anything wrong,* they "bind themselves with an oath, not in criminal conspiracy, but to abstain from fraud, banditry, and adultery, to commit no breach of trust, and not to renege on a deposit." He says that he tortured some of them to obtain the truth.[3] He finds out from those women who are called "ministers" that they meet together before dawn, sing hymns to Christ as to God (in Latin, they sing hymns *Christo quasi deo*), and they partake of a simple meal. He wants some advice from Trajan: how he is to take care of this growing menace that he thinks is going to be soon out of control, the growth of the number of Christians? Shall he continue his persecutions?

He gets a letter back from Trajan, which we also have. Trajan said, *You are doing right in order to forbid people from*

691–712; 772–87. For the full text of both letters, see: <http://www.kchanson.com/ANCDOCS/latin/pliny.html>.

[3] See Brunt, "Evidence Given under Torture in the Principate."

gathering together. The Roman empire was very nervous, and it laid down strict rules that no more than five people might congregate together in a public gathering because they were so deathly afraid of an uprising, either of slaves or of other people who were brought against their will into the empire. Authorities even did not permit fire brigades to exist. And in Bithynia there had been some very terrible fires that could not be quickly put out because they had disbanded the fire brigades on account of this law. These Christians would gather together before dawn, which suggests that many of the Christian believers that Peter writes to, who were in the second-generation church in Bithynia, were slaves, and the only free time was to get up while it was still dark. And they would meet together and have a simple meal; they would celebrate the Lord's supper, that is what that means. And they would sing hymns "to Christ as to God." Trajan happily puts the brakes on a certain kind of procedure that Pliny had been following: Pliny received anonymous declarations that such and such people are Christians. Trajan responds, "But anonymous accusations shall not be introduced into the proceedings. They set a bad precedent and are not in the spirit of our age." It is in this climate—already beginning in the second half of the first century, when this writer says,

> Beloved, do not be surprised at the fiery ordeal that is taking place among you to test you, as though something strange were happening to you. But rejoice insofar as you are sharing Christ's sufferings, so that you may also be glad and shout for joy when his glory is revealed. If you are reviled for the name of Christ, you are blessed, because the spirit of glory, which is the Spirit of God, is resting on you. But let none of you suffer as a murderer, or a thief, a criminal, or even as a mischief maker. Yet if any of you suffers as a Christian, do not consider it a

disgrace, but glorify God because you bear this
name. (1 Pet 4:12-16)

The word "Christian" occurs in only two books of the
New Testament. Only once here and twice in the book of
Acts.[4] The first is the statement that, "it was in Antioch [in
Syria] that the disciples were first called 'Christians'" (Acts
11:26). And the second time is when Agrippa is on the judgment seat, Paul is being tried, and Agrippa says, "Are you
so quickly persuading me to become a Christian ?" (Acts
26:28). The word "Christian" is not taken up by the writers of the New Testament. They do not regard it as a term
in which they can rejoice. They call themselves "disciples,"
"believers," "the saved." They call themselves the "followers
of Christ," but they are very slow about adopting the name
"Christian." It was a term of reproach. And it would have
been pronounced in a very malevolent way: "You Christians!" as though you were going to spit out the word. It was
not a term that they delighted in. It was only in the following generations, after the persecutions were over, that the
term "Christian" comes to be a term that you and I delight
to have and to own.

Now let me say in this connection that the relation of
the believers to the government was a very perilous situation.
And this letter takes into account that perilous situation by
laying down some very practical rules. In 1 Peter 2 and 3,
the writer provides a list of obligations that Christians have,
as to how they should live, individually and collectively. He
draws up for their guidance a number of practical sugges-
tions how, as individuals and as groups within a household,
they are to conduct themselves.

There were no church buildings at this time. In fact,
the earliest evidence that we have for the existence of a

---

[4] For a discussion of *christianoi*, see Elliott, *1 Peter,* 789–96; and
Wilkins, "Christian."

church sanctuary is from the early part of the third century.[5] In AD 201, there is evidence in a chronicle of Edessa that the rise of a river had gotten too close in the flood stage to the foundations of a church building, and the foundations of that church building were damaged. That is the first time, early third century, that we read of a church building. Where did these Christians meet? These Christians met in house-churches. They would meet in the homes of Christian believers in the community, and when the number of Christians grew so great, as at Corinth, then several different house-groups or churches would begin to function. Here, Peter is addressing Christian believers who are gathered in the circumstance of a home, worshipping.[6] And he has, therefore, some very practical advice about living conditions in the home. He says near the end of his letter, *Practice hospitality ungrudgingly to one another. As other Christians come to your community, open your home! Make available bed and breakfast,* we might put it. The hotels and taverns of that day were infested. They were infested with lice, with bandits, and with prostitutes. And traveling Christians would need the open-door policy on the part of Christian believers in this area, in that area. Well, these house-churches were the seed-plots for the growing church, and eventually, when separate buildings were constructed, then those who were already in the position of leadership in house-churches would probably be elected as elders and deacons, and other people put in charge of the running of a local congregation.

Martin Luther identified, as a running title at the top of the page of his German translation, the kind of list that we are about to look at now. Other New Testament letters

---

[5] See Snyder, *Ante Pacem.*

[6] On the phenomenon of house-churches, see Elliott, *A Home for the Homeless*; and Osiek and MacDonald, *A Woman's Place,* 68–94.

include similar lists, such as Colossians. He called them
Haustafeln, that is a household-table: a list of specifications
of how Christians should conduct themselves in the ordinary surroundings of the home.[7] This *Haustafeln* begins in
the broadest way: "For the Lord's sake accept the authority
of every human institution, whether of the emperor as supreme," that was Nero at this year that Peter was writing, "or
of governors," like Pliny would be, later on, "as sent by him
to punish those who do wrong and to praise those who do
right" (2:13-14). And then a very quick run-down: "Honor
everyone. Love the family of believers. Fear God. Honor
the emperor" (2:17). Very direct, practical directives. Now
he takes up successively different groups. First, servants or
slaves (2:18-25), then wives (3:1-6), followed by husbands
(3:7). In some of the other lists of *Haustafeln*, you have also
children mentioned (see Eph 6:1-4; Col 3:20).

Verses 18 and 20: "Slaves, accept the authority of your
masters with all deference, not only those who are kind and
gentle but also those who are harsh. . . . If you endure when
you are beaten for doing wrong, what credit is that? But if
you endure when you do right and suffer for it, you have
God's approval." And then he goes on to say, "you should
follow in his [Christ's] steps" (v. 21b). "When he [Christ]
was abused, he did not return abuse; when he suffered, he
did not threaten, but he entrusted himself to the one who
judges justly" (v. 23).

Peter addresses another group in chapter 3: "Wives,
in the same way, accept the authority of your husbands, so
that, even if some of them do not obey the word, they may
be won over without a word by their wives' conduct . . ." (3:1).
*Without constantly nagging, Won't you come to the church
service with me? Here's a pagan husband—what to do when*

[7] See, for example, Balch, *Let Wives Be Submissive*; and idem,
"Household Codes."

time comes for worship? Peter says, *The unconverted husband is more likely to be won by a wife without her words, when he sees her behavior, the reverent and chaste behavior. Let it be the hidden person of the heart rather than outward cosmetics that will be in God's sight very precious.* So says this writer, telling the wives, as he has told everybody, men and women alike; at the opening statement, in 2:13, he speaks to everyone: "accept the authority of every human institution."

You know, the wives at this time who were Christians had a particularly hard time of it. It was not only the custom, but it was written on the statute books of the laws, that the family had the same religion as the father or husband of the family. And so it would be only if the husband were tolerant that he would allow a Christian wife to associate herself with fellow Christian believers. More than once there would, undoubtedly, be harsh words and perhaps even violent physical blows administered to a wife that wanted to group herself with the Christians, and yet, who was kept under the thumb of her husband, and prevented from worshipping now "Christ as God."

Peter deals more at length now, in chapter 3, with the hard situation of the wives than he devotes to husbands in v. 7. That is understandable. The wives needed Peter's consoling words much more than the husbands needed Peter's directive to live considerately with their wives. Here was a case where it would have done absolutely no good in the world for Peter to have said, *Now you remember what Paul wrote, that "in Christ Jesus there is neither Jew nor Greek, there is neither slave nor free, there is neither male nor female; for all of you are one in Christ Jesus."* It would have done absolutely no good to tell that to the pagan husbands. They would say, *So what?* This is a difficult situation that Peter addresses, and I think we can see the Christian tact that Peter is involved in here, in dealing with that kind of situation. He could not just change the rules and the customs and the laws overnight. In this kind of situation, he says, "Wives, in the same way, accept the authority of your husbands, so that, even if some of them do not obey the word, they may be won over without a word by their wives' conduct, when they see the purity and reverence of your lives" (3:1-2).

Now with regard to husbands: "Likewise you husbands, live considerately with your wives, bestowing honor on the woman as the weaker sex" (3:7a). He is speaking here, probably, to relatively few Christian men, because at the outset it is likely that more women had been won to the gospel message than men. But for those who were Christian husbands, they are to bestow honor on the woman as the weaker sex. This is not to be taken that the women are inferior intellectually, spiritually, or in any other way. It is only that physically speaking, by and large, women are not as powerful in muscle as men are.

Notice how this verse (1 Peter 3:7) comes to an end in a wonderful way. "You are joint heirs of the grace of life." Christian husband and Christian wife are to live together, mutually heirs of eternal life, "so that nothing may hinder your prayers" (3:7b). What is the purpose of Christian marriage? It is to have a Christian family, progeny; it is for the mutual support of husband and wife. But here, the author states as the conclusion: Christian marriage is to enhance your spiritual life. "Show consideration . . . in order that your prayers may not be hindered." And now he gives a wrap-up. "Finally, all of you, have unity of spirit, sympathy, love for one another, a tender heart, and a humble mind" (3:8).

At the end of chapter 3 is a very difficult verse that exegetes have puzzled over for generations. Over the years I have studied it diligently, but I still do not know exactly to what 3:19 really refers. Christ "was put to death in the flesh, but made alive in the spirit" (3:18). Now vv. 19-20: "In which [spirit] he also went and made a proclamation to the spirits in prison, who in former times did not obey, when God waited patiently in the days of Noah, during the building of the ark, in which a few, that is, eight persons, were saved through water."

I have time only to enumerate briefly what the main theories are. Charles Hodge, James Orr (the Scottish theologian), and other Christian theologians and exegetes have taken this passage to mean that in the days of Noah, when the ark was being prepared, the preexistent Christ—Christ in the spirit—went and, through the mouth of Noah, proclaimed to Noah's contemporaries a message that they should repent.[8] The judgment was coming on the earth. It seems that that might be the meaning: Christ was put to death in the flesh but made alive in the spirit. In this spirit he went and preached to the spirits in prison, who formerly did not obey when God's patience waited in the days of Noah during the building of the ark.

A second way of understanding these opaque words is that they refer to the time between the death of Christ on Good Friday afternoon and his resurrection Easter Sunday morning; then in the spirit world he went and proclaimed to those who, back in the days of Noah, were condemned as sinners and now are held in the underworld, and receive now from the lips of the spirit Christ, during those three days he was in the grave, the message that Christ proclaimed to them. There are two divisions of this view. One is that Christ preached the gospel of redemption and offered them a second chance. The other view, that is more widespread, is that Christ reiterates in this three-day period a message of condemnation.

A third view has been suggested by a Jesuit theologian who did his doctoral dissertation at Rome on this verse,

---

[8] James Orr, "Prison, Spirits in"; see also Feinberg, "1 Peter 3:18-20."

William J. Dalton.[9] His view is that neither in the days of Noah nor during the three-day period that Christ was in Hades, but at the time of his ascension, returning to heaven, Christ the Exalted One proclaimed to the spirit beings in the heavenly places his message of triumph.

Let me say that sometimes I think the first explanation is the right one, while at other times I am persuaded by some of the arguments that support the second main view. I have not yet seen the validity of Father Dalton's third view. In other words, I do not know exactly what this means. But let me tell you, it had a great influence in following generations in the interpretation of the words in the Apostles' Creed: "Christ died, he was buried, he descended into hell. The third day he rose again from the dead. He ascended into heaven and sits at the right hand of God. From thence he will come to judge the quick and the dead." It had this influence whether rightly or wrongly; and I think that many people who make use of the words in the Apostles' Creed have a very wrong idea of what they are supposed to believe in terms of the word "hell." The word in the Greek rendering of the Apostles' Creed for hell is *hades*. The word in the Latin translation of the early Apostles' Creed ("he descended into hades") is the same word in Latin, *hades*.

This is a different place and condition from what is referred to twelve times in the New Testament as "Gehenna." Eleven of the twelve times that this word occurs in the New Testament come from the lips of Jesus. And he says that in Gehenna there is fire that is unquenchable and the worm that does not die. Gehenna is a place of punishment. The name *Gehenna* comes from two Hebrew words, *ge* and *hinnom,* "Valley of Hinnom," the valley south of Jerusalem, owned by a man named Hinnom, and hence called the valley of Hinnom. It was here that the dump was located for

[9] Dalton, *Christ's Proclamation to the Spirits.*

Jerusalem, where all of the garbage and the refuse and the carcasses of dead animals were disposed of. They would be thrown over the side and a fire would be started in order to prevent the putrefying mass from becoming overpowering in odor and in other disagreeable ways. The smoke that rises from Gehenna, if the wind was in the right direction, made everybody in Jerusalem aware of the existence of Gehenna. The worms and the maggots that feed on the decaying flesh flourish; they do not die. It becomes a term that indicates a place that you want to keep as far away from as possible. And Jesus makes use of that figure when he says, "And if your right hand causes you to sin, cut it off and throw it away; it is better for you to lose one of your members than for your whole body to go into [Gehenna]" (Matt 5:30).

Now getting back to what I started to say about the Apostles' Creed, "Christ descended into hades," which is not the same as Gehenna. Hades is not a place of punishment; it is not a place of fire and brimstone. Hades was a term that was used as the place of departed spirits, whether good or bad people. They all alike were in the place of departed spirits. And it is that which the Apostles' Creed has in mind. But when the Apostles' Creed was translated into English in the sixteenth century, the English word "hell" also had these two meanings: the place of departed spirits and the place of punishment and fire. In popular speech today, however, the word "hell" almost always means a place of punishment and of fire, and, therefore, it is built into the structure of our English vocabulary that people almost necessarily get the wrong understanding of what they are confessing in the words of the Apostles' Creed. How to avoid that is a great problem semantically. A few churches have introduced the statement "he descended into hades." But this seems so strange to some people that it is not very useful. I suppose the best thing is for pastors to explain to their congregation what exactly this means: *he descended into the place of departed spirits.*

Finally, that phrase was not added to the Apostles' Creed until the late fourth or early fifth Christian century. It was added, no doubt, to make sure that gnosticizing teaching would be corrected. This was added in order to underline that Christ really and truly died, was buried, and went to the place of departed spirits. Now, however, he has risen from the dead and has ascended to the right hand of God, and is seated there.

The phrase "He is at the right hand of God," finally, is an encouragement to you and me. What is the right hand of God? We do not believe that God has parts or passions. The right hand of God is a symbol for God's omnipotence. Where is God's right hand? Divine omnipotence is everywhere.

> If I ascend to heaven, you are there;
>> if I make my bed in Sheol, you are there.
> If I take the wings of the morning,
>> and settle at the farthest limits of the sea,
> even there your hand shall lead me,
>> and your right hand shall hold me fast.
> (Ps 139:8-10)

What does it mean, then, to sit at God's right hand? If God's right hand is divine omnipotence, where is it? It is everywhere! To sit at God's right hand means to wield the powers of divine omnipotence. Calvin said, "This is the language of princes." Why did Christ sit down? Is he tired? Does he not want to stand up anymore? He sits down because he is working. Monarchs sit on their thrones; they issue their sovereign decrees seated. Christ "sits at the right hand of God"; that is pictorial language, meaning that he now wields divine authority. "All authority in heaven and on earth has been given to me. Go therefore . . ." (Matt 28:18-19). That is saying in different words what Peter is saying here, and what the writer of the Letter to the Hebrews is saying in that work (1:13): that Christ is seated at the right hand of God. He is ruling as King of kings and Lord of lords. That is the message that comes through to us when we celebrate Ascension Day: Let us pray.

> *O Eternal God, who in the fullness of time sent forth thy Son, made of the woman, made under the Law, that He might redeem those that were under the Law, that we Gentiles might receive the adoption: We thank Thee that He is now ruling and reigning, and we pray that we may be loyal subjects of his. Looking to his will and conforming our plans to his great design for us in this life and in the life which is to come. In his name we pray. Amen.*

CHAPTER 3

The First Epistle of John

A Letter of Love

B Y EXPLORING these three apostolic letters of faith, hope, and love I have attempted to show what each of these letters has to say: both by way of the common doctrine of our holy Christian religion, and also through their differences. The differences arise naturally from the fact that three different individuals wrote these three letters. But there were also different problems that needed to be corrected in various parts of the Roman Empire. As we discuss 1 John, we will see yet a different problem that needed to be addressed by this apostolic writer.

When we look at the style of this letter, we see that it differs quite markedly from the style of Galatians (typical of Paul), and from the style of Peter—helped, no doubt, by Silvanus, his amanuensis, in his first epistle (1 Peter 5:12). The style of 1 John is the simplest in the whole of the New Testament. The range of vocabulary is quite limited. And the words that are used are simple, everyday words. And yet, the truths that are expressed in this letter are perhaps more profound truths about God than those found elsewhere in the New Testament.

The short treatise of 1 John is difficult to outline; in fact, although entitled a letter, it lacks the customary salutation of a letter. We do not know the name of the person who wrote it. And we do not know exactly the recipients for which it was originally intended. It lacks the beginning and the epistolary close that is normal in a letter. And yet, I think, early tradition is very likely correct in ascribing this anonymous letter to none other than the youngest of the twelve apostles. I conclude this based on three factors:

- early tradition
- the similarity to 2 John and 3 John in vocabulary and style, which do identify their author as the elder
- the similarity with the Gospel of John.

He lived the longest of any of the twelve apostles, perhaps into the middle 90s of the first century, as an elderly man, in charge of churches in and around Ephesus in Asia Minor.

He writes this letter for the purpose of deepening the spiritual life of his readers and for the purpose of correcting a heretical aberration that had begun to edge its way into the church at the close of the first century, namely, the heresy of Gnosticism, that very strange, theosophical speculation that, in this case, held that Jesus Christ was not truly incarnate in human flesh—that Jesus and Christ were, in fact, different beings.

Bishop Irenaeus, in his treatise against heresies,[1] warns against dividing Christ from Jesus, holding that at the baptism of the earthly Jesus, the heavenly Christ came down in the form of a dove. And then, just before crucifixion, the heavenly Christ left the earthly Jesus. An utterly bizarre idea was elaborated that the heavenly Christ took the twelve apostles to a hill near Jerusalem and pointed out how at that moment the Jews were crucifying Jesus. An early form of this appears in 1 John 4, where the author speaks against dividing Jesus and Christ, and says that "every spirit that confesses that Jesus Christ has come in the flesh is from God, and every spirit that does not confess Jesus is not from God. And this is the spirit of the antichrist" (1 John 4:2b-

[1] Robertson and Donaldson, editors, *Apostolic Fathers, Justin Martyr, Irenaeus.*

3a). The purpose of the author was to deepen the spiritual life of his readers and to warn against insidious heresy that would eviscerate the Christology articulated by Paul, Peter, James, John, Jude, and other New Testament writers.

Another thing that strikes us as we look at this passage is the author's idiosyncrasy of circling around a subject and looking at it from one point and then another. One who is not very much interested in this letter will think that it is very repetitious, because it goes around and around. But a careful reader will see that when the author circles around a subject, looking at it from different points of view, then the next time around it will be at a higher level and in a wider circle. If you describe this process by means of some sort of graph on a blackboard, it would be a spiral—a spiral that commences in a narrow way, and then widens the scope of looking at it, and each time around it ranges higher and higher.

Finally, another literary idiosyncrasy deserves mention. The author likes to make correlative statements. Again and again he puts together two things, saying, *It is this, and it is not that. You should do this and not that,* putting together pairs such as light and darkness, life and death. We will see, as we look at selected verses, how this feature is quite different from the style of Paul or Peter or any of the other New Testament writers. The Bible as a whole has a great deal to say about God and his activities: God creates, God sustains, God judges, God loves. Many verbs are used throughout the Scriptures regarding God's activities. But I remind you how infrequently in the Bible is there any statement as to what God is.

The apostle John, once in the Gospel, and twice in this letter, makes statements about the essence of God—what God is. He says, reporting the conversation of Jesus with the woman of Samaria, that God is spirit (John 4:24). That is a very profound statement and was necessary to correct the erroneous ideas held by the woman of Samaria as well as by many other people of the first century. They had the idea, inherited from centuries of belief, that God is localized. Think, for example, of the story about Elisha and Naaman, the captain of the army of the Syrians (2 Kings 5). After Elijah has healed Naaman's leprosy, Naaman asks for permission to take with him from Israel two muleloads of earth as he goes north into Syria, so that he can spread that earth from Israel on the ground and worship the God of Israel (2 Kgs 5:17).

People had the idea that God is somehow localized; and in the conversation of the woman of Samaria, she said, *Now, you Jews say that the right place to worship is in Jerusalem, Mt. Zion. We Samaritans, on the other hand, hold that it is right to worship God on Mt. Gerizim. What is your pronouncement on this theological problem?* And Jesus responds, "The hour is coming when neither on this mountain nor in Jerusalem will you worship the Father" (John 4:21), because God is spirit and not limited to time and geographical space. That was a major correction of an error held by many people in antiquity. God is not material, but spiritual, and those who worship him must worship him in spirit and in truth.

Now with this background, let us look at 1 John and see how its author teaches concerning the nature of God, as over against what God does. The essence of God is touched upon in this brief but very profound letter. The author begins with a very long sentence that extends from v. 1 to v. 3; and he breaks that sentence in v. 2 with a parenthesis. "We declare to you what was from the beginning, what we have heard, what we have seen with our eyes, what we have looked at and touched with our hands, concerning the word of life . . . ." Now he breaks off and inserts a parenthesis at v. 2 to define what he means by life. The word of life: "This life was revealed, and we have seen it and testify to it, and declare to you the eternal life that was with the Father and was revealed to us." Then he returns to the sentence that he had commenced in v. 1, with some reiteration, "We declare to you what we have seen and heard so that you also may have fellowship with us; and truly our fellowship is with the Father and with his Son, Jesus Christ."

This is a complicated sentence, unlike the rest of the sentences in the letter. But we can sort it out when we find the main subject and the main verb. The main subject we find in v. 3, namely, "We proclaim." That is the main thing that he is saying. Now he defines what he is proclaiming, starting with 1:1, "We declare to you what was from the beginning, what we have heard, what we have seen with our eyes, what we have looked at and touched with our hands, concerning the word of life," and this expanded parenthesis defines what that life is. *We proclaim that to you, also, as we have proclaimed it to many people. Now, to the readers of this letter we set forth the purpose*: "so that you also may have fellowship with us; and truly our fellowship is with the Father and with his Son, Jesus Christ." The purpose is to deepen their spiritual life (1:3).

These opening verses clamor for further attention. While I do not intend to devote much further attention to looking at individual terms and words, the expression "word of life" certainly demands comment. The Greek for the term "word" is *logos,* the same Greek word with which the Gospel of John commences, and proclaims "In the beginning was the Word [the *logos*], and the *logos* was with God, and the *logos* was God" (John 1:1). Of the forty meanings that the Greek lexicon of Liddell and Scott assign to the word *logos,* there are two primary areas: *Logos* means "that which is in the mind and the thought and the rationality"; and secondly, it means "that which is expressed verbally as a word."[2] Our author chooses this term to describe Christ,

---

[2] Liddell and Scott, *A Greek-English Lexicon,* 1057–59.

who was with the Father from the beginning, and who now is able, having been with the Father, to verbalize and issue forth in the incarnation and represent all that God is. It is this word of life that he says, *We testify to you and proclaim to you the eternal life.*

"God so loved the world that he gave his only Son, that whosoever believes in him might not perish, but have everlasting life" (John 3:16, KJV). "Everlasting life" is not as great a promise as "eternal life"; and the NRSV of John 3:16 translates the Greek word *aiōnios* by its more accurate rendering, "eternal life." Everlasting life is merely life without end; more of the same thing. But eternal life is life on a higher plane, a plane that is occupied by the Eternal One, God! It is a life that is different from a human, earthly life. Perhaps not everyone would want to have everlasting life of simply more and more of this life; but everyone will want to have the kind of life, the exhilarating life, of God. And that is eternal life—the life that is of a different quality from merely a greater quantity. This is the subject matter of the author: setting forth, proclaiming, the eternal life.

How does one outline this? Different commentators have different ways of dividing 1 John. I have found that the outline of this letter provided in the one-volume Bible commentary edited by the British author J. R. Dummelow is as helpful as any other outline.[3] Of course it is not up-to-date with regard to some of the more recent developments in New Testament research; but it focuses in a manner that few other one-volume commentaries do, namely, on the spiritual meaning of passages. In other words, I find it a very useful exegetical tool.

According to Dummelow, the outline of this brief letter is as follows: After the salutation the first section deals with the subject, "God is light" (1:5—2:28; see 1:5). The

---

[3] Dummelow, editor, *A Commentary on the Holy Bible.*

corollary of the statement that "God is light" is therefore that we Christian believers should walk in the light, as God is in the light. The second section deals with the subject, "God is righteous" (2:29—4:6; see 2:29). And the corollary, of course, is that because God is righteous, he expects his people to do righteous acts. And finally, and the most profound statement of all, "God is love" (4:7—5:12; see 4:8). The corollary is that we should show to one another a reflection of God's love, a love bestowed so abundantly upon us.

Now let us look at the contents of each of these three sections. "This is the message," he says, "we have heard from him and proclaim to you, that God is light and in him is no darkness at all" (1:5). Here we find for the first time the idiosyncrasy of a pair: "God is light and in him is no darkness." "If we say we have fellowship with him while we are walking in darkness, we lie and do not do what is true" (1:6); there is another balance. "But if we walk in the light, as he is in the light, we have fellowship with one another, and the blood of Jesus, his Son, cleanses us from all sin" (1:7).

In order to unpack the meaning of the statement "God is light," we must of course consider what light does and is in order to appreciate the analogous statement that "God is light." We use the term "light" in a variety of ways. We may speak, for example, of the physical realm when we say that light illuminates things. That is one characteristic of light; it does not remain confined. It spreads out and extends itself, and when we say "God is light," we are saying that God, in his nature, reveals himself, discloses himself, and does this supremely through Jesus Christ. But not only physically does light reflect the idea of the glory of God shining forth, but we talk about a person studying a problem as "seeing the light." Intellectually, light suggests the truth of God. Not just the glory of God, his splendor, but the truth of God is expressed by the term that "God is light." Finally, in the moral realm, not just physical, not just intellectual, but morally, light suggests the holiness of God.

The nature of God is set forth here in terms of the analogy: "God is light." Now that, in some ways, is similar to what Jesus said to the woman of Samaria, "God is spirit." But this transcends the earlier statement. This concentrates on the immateriality of God, but it concentrates on God's willingness and nature of disclosing himself, of imparting himself, of giving himself. Light, whether it is artificial light or light from the sun, streams forth. God is light. That wonderful truth is set forth at the beginning of this short letter, speaking to us, as the author goes on to say, underlining it, that we must live according to this light and truth.

The author of 1 John declares that if we confess our sins, "he who is faithful and just will forgive us our sins and cleanse us from all unrighteousness" (1:9). That promise is two-fold: "If we confess our sins, he who is faithful and just will forgive us our sins and cleanse us." We not only need pardon because we have offended God by sinning; we also need cleansing. A prisoner who may be pardoned at the bar of justice may still remain distorted in personality, filthy, and a totally disagreeable individual. Here the author talks about being freed from the chain of sin and being freed from the stain of sin. We are pardoned, forgiven, and cleansed by the blood of Jesus. "The blood of Jesus" is a shorthand expression, representing the entire ministry of Christ: his incarnation, his work of healing and teaching, the giving of himself and the shedding of his blood on the cross, his rising again, his ascension, and his present intercession on our behalf. Here then, our author says, "God is faithful and just, and will forgive us and cleanse us."

Finally, that God "is faithful and just" (1:9) is a kind of indirect blow against paganism, whose gods and goddesses were anything but faithful and just. The adulteries of Zeus, the chicaneries of Apollo—they were anything but faithful and just. "Faithful and just" is God, who has declared his purpose and does not swerve from it. It is not like a weather vane, which turns in every direction with every breath of wind. The pagan gods and goddesses of the pantheon at Olympus were not noted for being faithful and just. Here, in simple terms and without arguing, is a statement: our God is faithful; we can have confidence in him. He is just; he will do what is right.

Other issues clamor for attention, but we shall focus on a few verses in chapter 2 where the author says, "Do not love the world, or the things of the world. If anyone loves the world, love for the Father is not in him" (1 John 2:15). Here is a verse that describes the psychology of worldliness: "For all that is in the world, the lust of the flesh and the lust of the eyes and the pride of life, is not of the Father but is of the world" (1 John 2:16). Those three things consti-tute, he says, the essence of the psychology of worldliness. Kenneth Taylor, at this point in his paraphrase, *The Living Bible,* renders these familiar phrases in the following way: "Stop loving this evil world and all it offers you. . . . For all these worldly things, these evil desires—the craze for sex, the ambition to buy everything that appeals to you, and the pride that comes from wealth and importance—these are not from God."[4] This paraphrase focuses on the present-day understanding of what the psychology of worldliness is.

Later in chapter 2 is a word that occurs for the first time in the literature of the world. The word is "antichrist." No one ever, to our knowledge, had previously used the term "antichrist." The idea, however, was present. "Man of sin" is referred to by Paul in 2 Thessalonians 3:2, and other similar phrases such as "the man of sin" and "the man of lawlessness"; but the term "antichrist" now appears for the

[4] Taylor, *The Living New Testament.*

first time. The word is composed from the preposition *anti* and the word *Christ*. It has two chief meanings. It means, "A Christ that takes the place of the real Christ." It means, "a counterfeit Christ, a replacement." But it has a deeper malevolence than that. One football player may be sent in to take the place of another player, but they are not angry with each other. One may be a little disappointed when he is taken out of the team momentarily; but at any rate, there is a replacement. Antichrist is a replacement, a counterfeit; but the preposition *anti* means not only "another like the first," it means someone who is against the first, is an enemy, is an antagonist. An antichrist is someone who fights against Christ. "Children, it is the last hour," says our author; "and as you have heard that antichrist is coming, so now many antichrists have come; therefore we know it is the last hour" (2:18). The last days, the last hour, began already in the first century. The last days commence, says Peter in his sermon at Pentecost (Acts 2:17), quoting the prophecy of Joel, that "in the last days, I will pour out my Spirit upon all flesh." Now, with the coming of the Holy Spirit at Pentecost, Peter says, "The prophecy of Joel has been fulfilled. 'For, in the last days, I will pour out my spirit.'" Therefore, the period of the last days is not yet to come for us. It already is now. It commenced at Pentecost. We are still living in that last stage.

We now proceed to chapter 3 and mention some things that distress a number of people in the congregation. More than one person is distressed, perhaps, in reading "No one who abides in him sins; no one who sins has either seen him or known him" (3:6). And then "No one born of God commits sin; for God's nature abides in him, and he cannot sin because he is born of God" (3:9). These verses must be taken along with what the author says in chapter 1, when he says that, "If we say we have no sin, we deceive ourselves, and the truth is not in us" (1:8).

How do we reconcile these two things that seem dia-metrically opposed to each other? I think the simplest way is to consider the author's use of the present tense. In 1 John 3:6: "No one who abides in him [in Christ] sins." The present tense of continuing action. *No one who continually abides in Christ continually sins.* And v. 9: *No one born of God continually keeps on committing sin. But God's nature remains in him, and he cannot continually keep on sinning.* It is such a person who falls into occasional sin, and then asks God, who is faithful and just, to forgive us our sins. So the author underlines the tense in chapter 3—that this is the continuous tense in the Greek language. It is utterly incon-gruous that a Christian who says, *I am continually in Christ,* should continually live in sin—day in, day out. It would be as incongruous as if a member of a temperance society were continuously in a drunken stupor. That is to say, the incon-gruity is underlined in these verses in chapter 3.

The last topic, "God is love," is mentioned twice in chapter 4 of 1 John (vv. 8 and 16). There are four different Greek words that are translated into English by the verb "love." C. S. Lewis has a short book entitled *The Four Loves,* which deals with the four Greek words for *love.*[5] Two of these four words that are in the Greek vocabulary at large do not appear in the New Testament. One of them is the verb *storgeō* (noun, *storgē*), meaning "that special kind of love that is shown between a sovereign and his subjects." One does not often need to use that word, and the writers of the New Testament do not happen to use *storgeō.*

Another Greek word for "love" is *eraō* (noun, *eros*) from which "erotic" comes in English, sexual love. Now *eraō* in secular Greek had a wider import than merely the expression of sexual love, but perhaps the sexual nature was

[5] C. S. Lewis, *The Four Loves.*

so deeply imprinted on that word that New Testament writers avoid using it.

The third and fourth words in Greek meaning "love" are used frequently in the New Testament. *Phileō* (noun, *philia*) means to love with an affectionate sort of love. "Philadelphia" means "the city of brotherly love." A form of *phileō* is used sometimes meaning "to kiss." When Jesus was being arrested in Gethsemane, Judas went up to him and "he kissed him"; the verb is *kataphileō*. It expresses familiarity and affection.

Jesus also uses *phileō* when he castigates Pharisees who love to stand on the street corner and make a long prayer for pretense (Matt 6:5). So the verb *phileō* is sometimes a noble type and sometimes an ignoble type of expression of affection and behavior.

The verb *agapaō* (noun, *agapē*) is a fourth word meaning "love." It is a word that is used in John 3:16, "For God so loved the world." It is used in this letter, along with the noun, *agapē*. God is *agapē*. That kind of love is self-giving love, love that does not count the cost, love that is contrary to what you would expect! It is the kind of love that God is and that he exhibits.

Let us draw together some of these threads. God, according to the scriptures, does many things. He creates, he judges, he sustains, he loves. But when John says here, "God is love," that is a still more wonderful and profound statement, because all of God's activities are activities done in accordance with his nature, which is love. So when God's activity is that of creating, he creates according to his essence. According to his nature, he creates in love. When he sustains, he sustains you and me in love. It is according to his nature. When he judges, he judges in accordance with his nature. All that God does—and God's activity is referred to many times—is done in accordance with his nature, which involves self-giving love.

This Christian doctrine is so totally foreign to ancient philosophy that it is as light to darkness. One of the deepest of the ancient philosophers, Aristotle, said, "It is impossible that God should love." The author of 1 John declares that God *does* love, and in fact that God *is* love. It is this truth that John communicates through his brief letter—a letter that has been treasured down through the generations by members of the Christian church.

The letter comes to a conclusion in a simple but also in a profound way. It closes by saying, "Little children, keep yourselves from idols" (5:21). This elderly, last remaining disciple of our Lord regards the members of his churches as his spiritual children. He speaks to them with love and affection in the final sentence: "Little children, keep yourselves from idols." On every street corner in an ancient city, there would be a statue dedicated to Apollo, to Zeus, to Hera, to Juno, and so on. There were idols almost without number.

There are idols today. The goddess of lust, Venus, is not dead. The god of war, Mars, is not dead. The god of trickery and chicanery, Apollo, is not dead. We are to keep ourselves from these idols. The definition of an idol, and he warns against it, is anything that takes the place of God in our affections. Let us pray:

> *O Eternal God, how wonderful Thou art, past our finding out. We thank thee that we were not left to grope after thee, if happily we might find thee. But like light, thou dost disclose thyself in the person of thy Son. We pray that spiritually we may grow and worship thee, that in practical life in daily living, we may love thee, and love one another, and at last, do thou welcome us, we pray, into thy nearer presence, where we will be able to give thee a more perfect praise, world without end. In Christ's name, Amen.*

Conclusion

WE HAVE explored three apostolic letters of faith, hope, and love. Each of the authors is associated in the history of tradition with different parts of Christianity. Paul is especially emphasized by Protestants. Peter, prince of the apostles, is revered by Roman Catholics. John, emphasizing the spiritual and the mystical quality of our faith, has a special place among Eastern Orthodox Christians.

Faith, hope, and love. We can associate these with the past, the future, and the present. The past, faith, on which we anchor our commitment—we are justified by faith. The future is exemplified by hope—hope that that God, who has begun a good work in us, will surely bring it to completion at the appearing of his Son. And the present, love—letting others know that we have been with Jesus, and have learned of Him, showing forth in our lives the energy of love that comes from God to us, and comes from God to our neighbor. It is also the love that completes the triangle between us and our neighbor, the energy that finds its origin in God, to us and to others, now reciprocated between them and us, and back again, to love God with all our heart, soul, mind, and strength.

Paul tells the Corinthians that these three values are primary for Christians: "For now we see in a mirror dimly, but then face to face. Now I know in part; then I shall understand fully, even as I have been fully understood. So faith, hope, love abide, these three; but the greatest of these is love" (1 Cor 13:12-13). Our knowledge is incomplete.

Our understanding is often superficial. But we hold on to these fundamental values as Christ holds on to us in God's love.

❖ Select Bibliography

Ancient Epistles

Arzt, P. "The 'Epistolary Introductory Thanksgiving' in the Papyri and Paul." *NovT* 36 (1994) 29–46.

Aune, David. *The New Testament in Its Literary Environment*. LEC. Philadelphia: Westminster, 1987.

Bahr, Gregory J. "Paul and Letter Writing in the First Century." *CBQ* 28 (1966) 465–77.

———. "The Subscriptions in the Pauline Letters." *JBL* 87 (1968) 27–41.

Bradley, David. "The *Topos* as a Form in the Pauline *Paraenesis*." *JBL* 72 (1953) 238–46.

Cicero. *Letters to Quintus and Brutus; Letter Fragments; Letter to Octavian; Invectives; Handbook of Electioneering*. Edited and translated by D. R. Shackleton Bailey. LCL 462. Cambridge: Harvard University Press, 2002.

Deissmann, Adolf. *Light from the Ancient East: The New Testament Illustrated by Recently Discovered Texts of the Graeco-Roman World*. Translated by Lionel M. Strachen. Rev. ed. 1927. Reprinted, Eugene, Ore.: Wipf & Stock, 2004.

Dion, Paul. "The Aramaic 'Family Letter' and Related Epistolary Forms in Other Oriental Languages and in Hellenistic Greek." *Semeia* 22 (1982) 59–76.

Doty, William G. *Letters in Primitive Christianity*. GBS. Philadelphia: Fortress, 1973.

Elliott, John K. "The Language and Style of the Concluding Doxology to the Epistle to the Romans." *ZNW* 72 (1981) 124–30

Exler, Francis Xavier J. *The Form of the Ancient Greek Letter: A Study in Greek Epistolography*. 1923. Reprinted, Eugene, Ore.: Wipf & Stock, 2003.

Funk, Robert W. "The Apostolic *Parousia*: Form and Significance." In *Christian History and Interpretation: Studies Presented to John Knox*, edited by William R. Farmer, C. F. D. Moule,

R. R. Niebuhr, 249–68. Cambridge: Cambridge University Press, 1967.

Gamble, Harry Y. "Amanuensis." In *ABD* 1:172–73.

Hartman, Lars. "On Reading Others' Letters." *HTR* 79 (1986) 137–46.

Hout, Michiel van den. "Studies in Early Greek Letter-Writing." *Mnemosyne* 2 (1949) 19–43, 138–53.

Jewett, Robert. "The Epistolary Thanksgiving and the Integrity of Philippians." *NovT* 12 (1970) 40–53.

Longenecker, Richard N. "Ancient Amanuenses and the Pauline Epistles." In *New Dimensions in New Testament Study,* edited by Richard N. Longenecker and Merrill C. Tenney, 281–97. Grand Rapids: Zondervan, 1974.

Malherbe, Abraham J. *Ancient Epistolary Theorists.* SBLSBS 19. Missoula, Mont.: Scholars, 1988.

McGuire, M. R. P. "Letters and Letter Carriers in Christian Antiquity." *CW* 53 (1959–60) 148–53, 184–85, 199–200.

Meecham, Henry G. *Light from Ancient Letters: Private Correspondence in the Non-Literary Papyri of Oxyrhynchus of the First Four Centuries and Its Bearing on New Testament Language and Thought.* 1923. Reprinted, Eugene, Ore.: Wipf & Stock, 2004.

Metzger, Bruce M. "Stenography and Church History." In *Twentieth-Century Encyclopedia of the Religious Knowledge,* edited by Lefferts A. Loetscher, 1060–61. Grand Rapids: Baker, 1955.

Mitchell, Margaret M. "New Testament Envoys in the Context of Greco-Roman Diplomatic and Epistolary Conventions: The Example of Timothy and Titus." *JBL* 111 (1992) 641–62.

Mullins, Terence Y. "Formulas in New Testament Epistles." *JBL* 91 (1972) 380–90.

———. "Greeting as a New Testament Form." *JBL* 87 (1968) 418–26.

———. "Petition as a Literary Form." *NovT* 5 (1962) 46–54.

———. "*Topos* as a New Testament Form." *JBL* 99 (1980) 541–47.

O'Brian, Peter Thomas. *Introductory Thanksgivings in the Letters of Paul.* NovTSup 49. Leiden: Brill, 1977.

Purcell, Nicholas. "Postal Service." In *Oxford Classical Dictionary,* 3d ed., edited by Simon Hornblower and Antony Spawforth, 1233–34. Oxford: Oxford University Press, 1996.

Reed, Jeffrey T. "Are Paul's Thanksgivings 'Epistolary'?" *JSNT* 61 (1996) 87–99.

Roberts, J. H. "Pauline Transitions to the Letter Body." In *L'Apotre Paul: Personalite, Style et Conception du Ministere,* edited by A. Vanhoye, 93–99. Leuven: Peeters, 1986.

———. "Transitional Techniques to the Letter Body in the *Corpus Paulinum.*" In *A South African Perspective on the New Testament: Essays by South African New Testament Presented to Bruce Manning Metzger,* edited by J. H. Petzer and P. J. Hartin. Leiden: Brill, 1986.

Sanders, Jack T. "The Transition from Opening Epistolary Thanksgiving to Body in the Letters of the Pauline Corpus." *JBL* 71 (1962) 348–57.

Schubert, Paul. "Form and Function of the Pauline Letters." *JR* 19 (1939) 365–77.

Seneca. *Epistulae morales ad Lucilium.* 3 vols. Translated by R. M. Gummere. LCL. New York: Putnam, 1917–25.

Stirewalt, M. Luther Jr. "Paul's Evaluation of Letter-Writing." In *Search the Scriptures: New Testament Studies in Honor of Raymond T. Stamm,* edited by J. M. Myers et al., 179–96. GTS 3. Leiden: Brill, 1969.

———. *Studies in Ancient Greek Epistolography.* SBLRBS 27. Atlanta: Scholars, 1993.

Stowers, Stanley K. *Letter Writing in Greco-Roman Antiquity.* LEC. Philadelphia: Westminster, 1986.

———. "Letters (Greek and Latin)." In *ABD,* 4:290–93.

Tait, John G. "The Strategi and Royal Scribes in the Roman Period." *JEA* 8 (1922) 166–73.

Weima, Jeffrey A. D. *Neglected Endings: The Significance of the Pauline Letter Closings.* JSNTSup 101. Sheffield: JSOT Press, 1994.

Westermann, W. L. "On Inland Transportation and Communication in Antiquity." *PSQ* 43 (1928) 364–87.

White, John L. *The Form and Function of the Body of the Greek Letter: A Study of the Letter-Body in the Non-Literary Papyri and in Paul the Apostle.* 2d ed. SBLDS 2. Missoula, Mont.: Society of Biblical Literature, 1972.

———. "The Greek Documentary Letter Tradition Third Century B.C.E. to Third Century C.E." *Semeia* 22 (1982) 89–106.

———. "Introductory Formulae in the Body of the Pauline Letter." *JBL* 90 (1971) 91–97.

———. *Light from Ancient Letters.* Foundations and Facets. Philadelphia: Fortress, 1986.

————. "New Testament Epistolary Literature in the Framework of Ancient Epistolography." In *ANRW* II.25.2 (1984) 1730–56.

————. "Saint Paul and the Apostolic Letter Tradition." *CBQ* 45 (1983) 433–44.

Zilliacus, Laurin. *From Pillar to Post: The Troubled History of the Mail.* London: Heinemann, 1956.

Galatians

Commentaries

Betz, Hans Dieter. *Galatians.* Hermeneia. Philadelphia: Fortress, 1979.

Bruce, F. F. *The Epistle of Paul to the Galatians: A Commentary on the Greek Text.* NIGTC. Grand Rapids: Eerdmans, 1982.

Burton, Ernest de Witt. *Galatians.* ICC. Edinburgh: T. & T. Clark, 1921.

Calvin, John. *Commentaries on the Epistles of Paul to the Galatians and Ephesians.* Translated by William Pringle. Grand Rapids: Eerdmans, 1948.

Longenecker, Richard N. *Galatians.* WBC 41. Waco: Word, 1990.

Lührmann, Dieter. *Galatians.* Translated by O. C. Dean. CC. Minneapolis: Augsburg, 1992.

Malina, Bruce J., and John J. Pilch. *Social-Science Commentary on the Letters of Paul.* Minneapolis: Fortress, 2006.

Martyn, J. Louis. *Galatians.* AB 33A. New York: Doubleday, 1997.

Matera, Frank. *Galatians.* SacPag 9. Collegeville, Minn.: Liturgical, 1992.

Perkins, Pheme. *Abraham's Divided Children: Galatians and the Politics of Faith.* NTC. Harrisburg: Trinity, 2001.

Studies

Barrett, C. K. *Freedom and Obligation: A Study of the Epistle to the Galatians.* Philadelphia: Westminster, 1985.

Betz, Hans Dieter. "Galatians, Epistle of." In *ABD* 2:872–75.

————. "The Literary Composition and Function of Paul's Letter to the Galatians." *NTS* 21 (1975) 353–79.

Craffert, Pieter F. "Paul's Damascus Experience as Reflected in Galatians 1: Call or Conversion?" *Scriptura* 29 (1989) 36–47.

Dunn, James D. G. *Jesus, Paul and the Law: Studies in Mark and Galatians.* Louisville: Westminster John Knox, 1990.

Elliott, John H. "Paul, Galatians, and the Evil Eye." *CTM* 17 (1990) 262–73.

Esler, Philip F. "Making and Breaking an Agreement Mediterranean Style: A New Reading of Galatians 2.1-14." *BibInt* 3 (1995) 285–314.

———. "Family Imagery and Christian Identity in Gal. 5.13—6.10." In *Constructing Early Christian Families: Family as Social Reality and Metaphor,* edited by Halvor Moxnes, 121–49. London: Routledge, 1997.

———. *Galatians.* NTR. London: Routledge, 1998.

Gaventa, Beverly Roberts. "Galatians 1 and 2: Autobiography as Paradigm." *NovT* 28 (1986) 309–26.

Hall, Robert G. "The Rhetorical Outline for Galatians: A Reconsideration." *JBL* 106 (1987) 277–87.

Hanson, A. T. "The Origin of Paul's Use of *Paidagogos* for the Law." *JSNT* 34 (1988) 71–76.

Hays, Richard B. *The Faith of Jesus Christ: An Investigation of the Narrative Substructure of Galatians 3:1—4:11.* SBLDS 56. Chico, Calif.: Scholars, 1983.

Howard, George. *Paul: Crisis in Galatia—A Study in Early Christianity.* 2d ed. SNTSMS 35. Cambridge: Cambridge University Press, 1990.

Jewett, Robert. "The Agitators and the Galatian Congregation." *NTS* 17 (1970–71) 213–26.

Lambrecht, Jan. "Paul's Reasoning in Galatians 2.11-21." In *Paul and the Mosaic Law: The Third Durham–Tübingen Research Symposium on Earliest Christianity and Judaism (Durham, September 1994),* edited by James D. G. Dunn, 53–74. WUNT 89. Tübingen: Mohr/Siebeck, 1996.

———. "Transgressor by Nullifying God's Grace: A Study of Galatians 2.18-21." *Bib* 72 (1991) 217–36.

Lull, David J. "The Law Was Our Pedagogue: A Study in Galatians 3.19-25." *JBL* 105 (1986) 481–98.

———. *The Spirit in Galatia: Paul's Interpretation of Pneuma as Divine Power.* SBLDS 49. 1980. Reprinted, Eugene, Ore.: Wipf & Stock, 2006.

Martyn, J. Louis. "A Law-Observant Mission to Gentiles: The Background of Galatians." *SJT* 38 (1986) 307–24.

Metzger, Bruce M. *The New Testament: Its Background, Growth and Content.* 3d ed. Nashville: Abingdon, 2003.

Nanos, Mark D., editor. *The Galatians Debate: Contemporary Issues in Rhetorical and Historical Interpretation.* Peabody, Mass.: Hendrickson, 2002.

———. *The Irony of Galatians: Paul's Letter in First-Century Context.* Minneapolis: Fortress, 2002.

Neyrey, Jerome H. "Bewitched in Galatia: Paul's Accusation of Witchcraft." In idem, *Paul in Other Words: A Cultural Reading of His Letters,* 181–206. Louisville: Westminster John Knox, 1990.

———. "Theologies in Conflict: Paul's God in Galatians." In idem, *Render to God: New Testament Understandings of the Divine,* 191–211. Minneapolis: Fortress, 2004.

Riches, John K. "Galatians, Book of." In *Dictionary for Theological Interpretation of the Bible,* edited by Kevin Vanhoozer, 238–42. Grand Rapids: Eerdmans, 2005.

Stanton, Graham. "The Law of Moses and the Law of Christ, Galatians 3.1—6.2." In *Paul and the Mosaic Law: The Third Durham–Tübingen Research Symposium on Earliest Christianity and Judaism (Durham, September 1994),* edited by James D. G. Dunn, 99–116. WUNT 89. Tübingen: Mohr/Siebeck, 1996.

Tomson, Peter J. *Paul and the Jewish Law: Halakha in the Letters of the Apostle to the Gentiles.* CRINT III/1. Minneapolis: Fortress, 1990.

Verseput, Donald J. "Paul's Gentile Mission and the Jewish Christian Community: A Study of the Narrative in Galatians 1 and 2." *NTS* 39 (1993) 36–58.

Weima, Jeffrey A. D. "Gal. 6:11-18: A Hermeneutical Key to the Galatian Letter." *CTJ* 28 (1993) 90–107.

Wiley, Tatha. *Paul and the Gentile Women: Reframing Galatians.* New York: Continuum, 2005.

Wright, N. T. "Gospel and Theology in Galatians." In *Gospel in Paul: Studies on Corinthians, Galatians and Romans for Richard N. Longenecker,* edited by L. Ann Jervis and Peter Richardson, 222–39. JSNTSup 108. Sheffield: Sheffield Academic, 1994.

Young, Norman H. "*Paidagogos:* The Social Setting of a Pauline Metaphor." *NovT* 29 (1987) 150–76.

1 Peter

Commentaries

Achtemeier, Paul J. *1 Peter.* Hermeneia. Minneapolis, 1996.

Beare, F. W. *The First Epistle of Peter.* 3d ed. Oxford: Blackwell, 1970.

Boring, M. Eugene. *1 Peter.* ANTC. Nashville: Abingdon, 1999.

Davids, Peter H. *The First Epistle of Peter.* NICNT. Grand Rapids: Eerdmans, 1990.

Elliott, John H. *1 Peter.* AB 37B. New York: Doubleday, 2000.

Horrell, David G. *The Epistles of Peter and Jude.* EpComm. Peterborough: Epworth, 1998.

Jobes, Karen H. *1 Peter.* BECNT. Grand Rapids: Baker, 2005.

Kelly, J. N. D. *A Commentary on the Epistles of Peter and Jude.* New York: Harper & Row, 1969.

Michaels, J. Ramsey. *1 Peter.* WBC 49. Waco: Word, 1988.

Perkins, Pheme. *First and Second Peter, James, and Jude.* IBC. Louisville: Westminster John Knox, 1995.

Studies

Balch, David L. *Let Wives Be Submissive: The Domestic Code in 1 Peter.* SBLDS 26. Atlanta: Scholars, 1981.

———. "Household Codes." In *ABD* 3:318–20.

Bechtler, Steven Richard. *Following in His Steps: Suffering, Community, and Christology in 1 Peter.* SBLDS 162. Atlanta: Scholars, 1998.

Campbell, Barth L. *Honor, Shame, and the Rhetoric of 1 Peter.* SBLDS 162. Atlanta: Scholars, 1998.

Dalton, William J. *Christ's Proclamation to the Spirits: A Study of 1 Peter 3:18—4:6.* 2d ed. AnBib 23. Rome: Pontifical Biblical Institute Press, 1989. 1st ed. 1965.

Danker, Frederick W. "I Peter 1:24—2:17, A Consolatory Pericope." *ZAW* 58 (1967) 93–102.

Elliott, John H. "Disgraced Yet Graced: The Gospel According to 1 Peter in the Key of Honor and Shame." *BTB* 25 (1995)166–78.

———. *The Elect and the Holy: An Exegetical Examination of 1 Peter 2:4-10 and the Phrase* Basileion Hierateuma. NovTSup 12. 1966. Reprinted, Eugene, Ore.: Wipf & Stock, 2006.

————. *A Home for the Homeless: A Social-Scientific Criticism of 1 Peter, Its Situation and Strategy with a New Introduction.* Minneapolis: Fortress, 1990. Reprinted, Eugene, Ore.: Wipf & Stock, 2005.

————. "Peter, First Epistle of." In *ABD* 5:269–78.

————. "Peter, Silvanus and Mark in 1 Peter and Acts: Sociological-Exegetical Perspectives on a Petrine Group in Rome." In *Wort in der Zeit: Neutestamentliche Studien. Festgabe für Karl Heinrich Rengstorf zum 75. Geburtstag,* edited by Wilfrid Haubeck and Michael Bachmann, 250–67. Leiden: Brill, 1980.

————. "The Rehabilitation of An Exegetical Step-Child: 1 Peter in Recent Research." *JBL* 95 (1976) 243–54.

Feinberg, John S. "1 Peter 3:18-20, Ancient Mythology, and the Intermediate State." *WTJ* 48 (1986) 303–36.

Martin, Ralph P. "1 Peter." In *The Theology of the Letters of James, Peter, and Jude,* A. Chester and R. P. Martin, 87–133. NTT. Cambridge: Cambridge University Press, 1994.

Martin, Troy W. *Metaphor and Composition in 1 Peter.* SBLDS 131. Atlanta: Scholars, 1992.

Moule, C. F. D. "The Nature and Purpose of 1 Peter." *NTS* 3 (1955–56) 1–11.

Orr, James. "Prison, Spirits in." In *ISBE* 4:2456–57.

Piper, J. "Hope as the Motivation of Love: 1 Peter 3:9-12." *NTS* 26 (1978–79) 212–31.

Rodgers, Peter R. "1 Peter, Book of." In *Dictionary for Theological Interpretation of the Bible,* edited by Kevin Vanhoozer, 581–83. Grand Rapids: Eerdmans, 2005.

Schutter, W. L. *Hermeneutic and Composition in 1 Peter.* WUNT 2/30. Tübingen: Mohr/Siebeck, 1989.

Seland, Torrey. "The 'Common Priesthood' of Philo and 1 Peter: A Philonic Reading of 1 Peter 2.5, 9." *JSNT* 57 (1995) 87–119.

Talbert, Charles H., editor. *Perspectives on First Peter.* Macon, Ga.: Mercer University Press, 1986.

Thurén, Lauri. *Argument and Theology in 1 Peter: The Origins of Christian Paraenesis.* SBLDS 114. Atlanta: Scholars, 1985.

Volf, Miroslav. "Soft Difference: Theological Reflections on the Relation between Church and Culture in 1 Peter." *Ex Auditu* 10 (1994) 15–30.

1 John

Commentaries

Brown, Raymond E. *The Epistles of John*. AB 30. Garden City, N.Y.: Doubleday, 1982.

Bruce, F. F. *The Epistles of John*. Grand Rapids: Eerdmans, 1970.

Bultmann, Rudolf. *The Johannine Epistles*. Translated by R. Philip O'Hara et al. Hermeneia. Philadelphia: Fortress, 1973.

Dodd, C. H. *The Johannine Epistles*. MNTC. New York: Harper, 1946.

Kysar, Robert. *I, II, III John*. AugCNT. Minneapolis: Augsburg, 1986.

Marshall, I. Howard. *The Epistles of John*. NICNT. Grand Rapids: Eerdmans, 1978.

Painter, John. *1, 2, and 3 John*. SacPag 18. Collegeville, Minn.: Liturgical, 2002.

Rensberger, David. *1 John, 2 John, 3 John*. ANTC. Nashville: Abingdon, 1997.

Schnackenburg, Rudolf. *The Johannine Epistles*. Translated by Reginald Fuller and Ilse Fuller. New York: Crossroad, 1992.

Smalley, Stephen S. *1, 2, 3 John*. WBC 51. Waco: Word, 1984.

Smith, D. Moody. *First, Second and Third John*. IBC. Louisville: Westminster John Knox, 1991.

Strecker, Georg. *The Johannine Letters: A Commentary on 1, 2, and 3 John*. Translated by Linda M. Maloney. Hermeneia. Minneapolis: Fortress, 1996.

Thompson, Marianne Meye. *1–3 John*. IVPNTCS. Downers Grove, Ill.: InterVarsity, 1992.

Studies

Brown, Raymond E. *The Community of the Beloved Disciple*. New York: Paulist, 1979.

Callahan, Allen D. *A Love Supreme: A History of the Johannine Tradition*. Minneapolis: Fortress, 2005.

Culpepper, R. Alan. *The Johannine School: An Evaluation of the Johannine-School Hypothesis Based on an Investigation of the Nature of Ancient School*. SBLDS 26. Missoula, Mont.: Scholars, 1975.

Griffith, Terry. *Keep Yourselves from Idols: A New Look at 1 John.* JSNTSup 233. London: Sheffield Academic, 2002.

Hills, Charles E. *The Johannine Corpus in the Early Church.* Oxford: Oxford University Press, 2004.

Hills, Julian V. "A Genre for 1 John." In *The Future of Early Christianity: Essays in Honor of Helmut Koester,* edited by Birger A. Pearson et al., 367–77. Minneapolis: Fortress, 1991.

Marshall, I. Howard. "Johannine Epistles." In *Dictionary for Theological Interpretation of the Bible,* edited by Kevin Vanhoozer, 391–94. Grand Rapids: Eerdmans, 2005.

Lieu, Judith. *The Theology of the Johannine Epistles.* NTT. Cambridge: Cambridge University Press, 1991.

Perkins, Pheme. "*Koinonia* in 1 John 1:3-7: The Social Context of Division in the Johannine Letters." *CBQ* 45 (1983) 631–41.

Segovia, Fernando F. *Love Relationships in the Johannine Tradition: Agape/Agapan in I John and the Fourth Gospel.* SBLDS 58. Chico, Calif.: Scholars, 1982.

———. "Recent Research in the Johannine Letters." *RSR* 13 (1987) 132–39.

Watson, Duane F. "Amplification Techniques in 1 John: The Interaction of Rhetorical Style and Invention." *JSNT* 51 (1993) 99–123.

Additional References

The Authorized Daily Prayer Book of the United Hebrew Congregations of the British Commonwealth of Nations. Translated by S. Singer. 2d rev. ed. London: Eyre & Spottiswoode, 1962.

Bartchy, S. Scott. "Community of Goods in Acts." In *The Future of Early Christianity: Essays in Honor of Helmut Koester,* edited by Birger A. Pearson et al., 309–18. Minneapolis: Fortress, 1991.

———. "Table Fellowship." In *Dictionary of Jesus and the Gospels,* edited by Joel Green and Scot McKnight, 796–800. Downers Grove, Ill.: InterVarsity, 1992.

Brunt, P. A. "Evidence Given under Torture in the Principate." *Zeitschrift der Savigny-Stiftung für Rechtsgeschichte* 97 (1980) 256–65.

Calvin, John. *Calvin: Institutes of the Christian Religion.* 2 vols. Edited by John T. McNeil. Translated by Ford Lewis Battles. Library of Christian Classics 21. Philadelphia: Westminster, 1960.

Deissmann, Adolf. *Die neutestamentliche Formel "in Christo Jesus."* Marburg: Elwert, 1892.

———. *St. Paul: A Study in Social and Religious History.* Translated by Lionel R. M. Strachan. New York: Hodder and Stoughton, 1912.

Dummelow, J. R., editor, *A Commentary on the Holy Bible.* London: Macmillan, 1909.

Dunn, James D. G. *The Theology of Paul the Apostle.* Grand Rapids: Eerdmans, 1998.

Jeremias, Joachim. "Paul and James." *ExpT* 66 (1954) 368–71.

Kierkegaard, Søren. *The Present Age; and, Of the Difference between a Genius and an Apostle.* Translated by Alexander Dru, Introduction by Walter Kaufmann. New York: Harper & Row, 1962.

Lewis, C. S. *The Four Loves.* New York: Harcourt Brace, 1960.

Liddell, H. G., and Robert Scott, *A Greek-English Lexicon.* Revised and augmented by Henry Stuart Jones, Roderick McKenzie et al. Oxford: Clarendon, 1996.

Luther, Martin. *Lectures on Galatians 1535, Chapter 1–4.* Translated by Jaroslav Pelikan. *Luther's Works* 26. St. Louis: Concordia, 1963.

Metzger, Bruce M. *The Canon of the New Testament: Its Origin, Development, and Significance.* Oxford: Clarendon, 1987.

Norris, Frederick W. "Antioch of Syria." In *ABD* 1:265–69.

Osiek, Carolyn, and Margaret Y. MacDonald, with Janet H. Tulloch. *A Woman's Place: House Churches in Earliest Christianity.* Minneapolis: Fortress, 2006.

Robertson, Alexander, and James Donaldson, editors. *Apostolic Fathers, Justin Martyr, Irenaeus.* Ante-Nicene Fathers 1. Peabody, Mass.: Hendrickson, 1994.

Sandwell, Isabella, and Janet Huskinson, editors. *Culture and Society in Later Roman Antioch: Papers from a Colloquim, London, 15th December 2001.* Oakville, Conn.: Brown, 2004.

Schnelle, Udo. *Apostle Paul: His Life and Theology.* Translated by Eugene M. Boring. Grand Rapids: Baker, 2005.

Sherwin-White, A. N. *The Letters of Pliny: A Social and Historical Commentary.* Oxford: Clarendon, 1966.

Snyder, Graydon F. *Ante Pacem: Archaeological Evidence of Church Life before Constantine.* Rev. ed. Macon, Ga.: Mercer University Press, 2003.

Stout, Selatie Edgar. *Plinius, Epistulae: A Critical Edition.* Bloomington: Indiana University Press, 1962.

Taylor, Kenneth N. *The Living New Testament.* Wheaton, Ill.: Tyndale, 1967.

Wilkins, Michael J. "Christian." In *ABD* 1:925–26.

Scripture Index